THE
German
TRAVELMATE

compiled by LEXUS
with Ingrid Schumacher

American Advisory Board:
Dr. John C. Traupman
Miles Turner
Jeanne Preston Whitman

Golden Press • New York
Western Publishing Company, Inc.
Racine, Wisconsin

Published by Golden Press, New York, New York

First Published in Great Britain by
Richard Drew Publishing Ltd. 1982

© Richard Drew Publishing Ltd. and
Lexus Ltd. 1983, 1982

All rights reserved. No part of this book may be
reproduced or copied in any form without written
permission from the publisher. Printed in the U.S.A.
Library of Congress Catalog Card Number: 82-83996

Golden® and Golden Press® are trademarks of
Western Publishing Company, Inc.
ISBN 0-307-46603-5

Your **Golden Travelmate** gives you one easy alphabetized list of both English and German words and phrases. Everything you need to communicate in German is here. Look up a word you want to say and besides finding the German word, often you'll find the word used in several questions or statements. In this list you'll also find:

- German words you'll see on signs
- Typical replies to questions you might be asked
- Translations of typical replies to your questions
- Travel Tips to help you get around and understand German customs
- Menu Interpreter (pages 72–73)

The German alphabet is on page 127 and numbers are on page 128.

PRONOUNCING GERMAN
Your **Golden Travelmate** also tells you how to pronounce German. Just read the pronunciations as though they were English, and you will be able to communicate – although you may not sound like a native speaker.

There are some special sounds:

oo is like oo in 'soon'
oo is like oo in 'book'
oo is similar to the u sound in 'huge'
ow is like ow in 'cow'
k is like the ch in 'yuch'

If no pronunciation is given, then the word itself can be spoken as though it were English. Sometimes only part of a word or phrase needs a pronunciation guide. Vowels in italics show which part of a word to stress.

a, an ein, eine, ein [ine, ine-uh, ine]
there are three genders in German: masculine, feminine and neuter; see also **the**
Abfahrt *departures*
aboard an Bord [bort]
about: about 15 ungefähr fünfzehn [oon-gheh-fair foonf-tsayn]
  at about 2 o'clock gegen zwei Uhr [gay-ghen tsvy oor]
above über [ōōber]
  above that darüber [da-rōōber]
abroad im Ausland [im ōwss-lannt]
absolutely! genau! [gheh-nōw]
absorbent cotton die Watte [vattuh]
accept annehmen [an-nay-men]
accident der Unfall [oonfal]
  there's been an accident es ist ein Unfall passiert [... pas-*ee*-ert]
accommodations die Unterkunft [oonter-koonft]
  we need accommodations for three wir brauchen Zimmer für drei [veer brōw-*k*en tsimmer foor dry]
» *TRAVEL TIP: as well as hotels there is the 'Hotel Garni' (bed and breakfast), 'Pension' (boarding house), 'Gasthof' (inn) or a room in a private house; look for the sign 'Zimmer frei' or 'Fremdenzimmer'; information on local accommodations from railroad station, look for 'Zimmernachweis' or tourist information office*
accountant ein Wirtschaftsprüfer [veert-shaffts-prōōfer]
accurate genau [gheh-nōw]

6 ACHE

ache der Schmerz [shmairts]
  my back aches ich habe Rückenschmerzen
  [ish hah-buh rōocken-shmairtsen]
Achtung *caution, danger; (spoken)* **look out!**
  (announcement) **attention please**
across über [ōober]
  how do we get across? wie kommen wir
  hinüber? [vee . . . veer]
ad die Annonce [a-non-suh]
***ADAC Allgemeiner Deutscher Automobil-
Club*** *equivalent of AAA*
adapter *(electrical)* der Zwischenstecker
  [tsvishen-sht–]
address die Adresse [ad-ressuh]
  will you give me your address? würden Sie
  mir Ihre Adresse geben? [vōorden zee meer
  eeruh ad-ress-uh gay-ben]
admission der Eintritt [ine–]
advance: in advance im voraus [im for-ōwss]
  can we make advance reservations?
  können wir im voraus buchen? [kurrnen
  veer . . . boo-ken]
afraid: I'm afraid I don't know das weiß ich
  leider nicht [. . . vice ish ly-duh . . .]
  I'm afraid so ja, leider
  I'm afraid not leider nicht
after: after you nach Ihnen [nahk ee-nen]
  after 2 o'clock nach zwei Uhr
afternoon der Nachmittag [nahk-mi-tahg]
  in the afternoon nachmittags [–tahgs]
  this afternoon heute nachmittag
  [hoy-tuh . . .]
  good afternoon guten Tag! [goo-ten tahg]
after-shave das Rasierwasser [raz-eer-vasser]
again wieder [veeder]
against gegen [gay-ghen]
age das Alter [al-ter]
  it takes ages das dauert eine Ewigkeit
  [. . . dōwert ine-uh ay-vish-kite]
agent der Vertreter [fair-tray-ter]
ago: a week ago vor einer Woche [for ine-uh
  vockuh]

ALONE 7

it wasn't long ago das ist noch nicht lange her [dass ist no*k* nisht lang-uh hair]
how long ago was that? wie lange ist das her? [vee . . .]
agree: I agree da stimme ich zu [. . . shtimmuh ish tsoo]
it doesn't agree with me das bekommt mir nicht [. . . buh-kommt meer nisht]
air die Luft [l∞ft]
by air per Flugzeug [pair floog-tsoyg hair]
with air conditioning mit Klimaanlage [. . . kleema-an-lahguh]
by airmail per Luftpost [pair l∞ft-posst]
airplane das Flugzeug [floog-tsoyg]
airport der Flughafen [floog-hah-fen]
alarm der Alarm
alarm clock der Wecker [v–]
alcohol der Alkohol [–hohl]
is it alcoholic? ist das Alkohol?
alive lebendig [lay-b*e*n-dish]
is he still alive? lebt er noch? [laypt air no*k*]
all: all the people alle Leute [al-uh loy-tuh]
all night/all day die ganze Nacht/den ganzen Tag [dee gants-uh nah*k*t/dayn gants-en tahg]
that's all wrong das ist ganz falsch
all right! in Ordnung! [. . . ort-n∞ng]
that's all das ist alles [. . . al-ess]
thank you – not at all danke – bitte [bittuh]
allergic: I'm allergic to . . . ich bin allergisch gegen . . . [. . . al-air-ghish gay-ghen]
allowed erlaubt [air-lōwpt]
is it allowed? darf man das?
it's not allowed das ist verboten! [fair-boh-ten]
allow me gestatten Sie mir [gheh-sht*a*t-ten zee meer]
almost fast [fasst]
alone allein [al-*i*ne]
did you come here alone? sind Sie allein hier? [zinnt zee . . . heer]

8 ALPS

leave me alone lassen Sie mich in Ruhe! [... zee mish in roo-uh]
Alps die Alpen
already schon [shohn]
also auch [ōwk]
alternator die Lichtmaschine [lisht-mash-ee-nuh]
although obwohl [ob-vohl]
altogether insgesamt [ints-gheh-zammt]
always immer
a.m. vormittags [for-mi-tahgs]
ambassador der Botschafter [boht-shaffter]
ambulance der Krankenwagen [kranken-vah-ghen]
 get an ambulance! rufen Sie einen Krankenwagen! [roo-fen zee ine-en ...]
» *TRAVEL TIP: dial 110*
America Amerika [am-ay-ree-kah]
American amerikanisch
 (person) ein Amerikaner
 (woman) eine Amerikanerin
 Americans die Amerikaner
 I'm American ich bin Amerikaner/Amerikanerin
among unter [oonter]
amp das Ampere [am-pair]
and und [oont]
angry böse [burr-zuh]
 I'm very angry about it ich bin darüber sehr verärgert [... darōōber zair fair-air-ghert]
 please don't get angry seien Sie bitte nicht böse! [zy-en zee bittuh ...]
animal das Tier [teer]
ankle der (Fuß)knöchel [fōossk-nurr-shell]
Ankunft arrivals
Anlieger frei residents only
Anmeldung reception
anniversary: it's our wedding anniversary heute ist unser Hochzeitstag [hoy-tuh ist oon-zer hohk-tsites-tahg]
annoy: he's annoying me er belästigt mich [air bell-est-isht mish]

APPLICATION FORM 9

it's very annoying das ist sehr ärgerlich [dass ist zair air-gherlish]
another: may we have another room? können wir ein anderes Zimmer haben? [kurrnen veer ine an-dress tsimmer hah-ben]
another beer, please noch ein Bier, bitte [no*k* ine beer bittuh]
answer die Antwort [ant-vort]
what was his answer? was hat er darauf geantwortet? [vass hat air da-rōwf gheh-*a*nt-vortet]
there was no answer *(tel)* es hat sich niemand gemeldet [... zish nee-mannt gheh–]
antifreeze der Frostschutz [–sh*oo*ts]
any: do you have any bananas/butter? haben Sie Bananen/Butter? [hah-ben zee ba-nah-nen/b*oo*-ter]
I don't have any hab' ich nicht [hahb ish nisht]
anybody (irgend) jemand [eer-ghent yay-mannt]
can anybody help? kann jemand helfen?
anything (irgend)etwas [eer-ghent et-vass]
I don't want anything ich möchte gar nichts [ish murrshtuh gahr nix]
apartment eine Wohnung [voh-n*oo*ng]
aperitif ein Aperitif
apology eine Entschuldigung [ent-sh*oo*l-dee-g*oo*ng]
please accept my apologies bitte, verzeihen Sie mir [bittuh fair-tsy-en zee meer]
I want an apology ich warte auf eine Entschuldigung [... vartuh ōwf ine-uh ...]
appendicitis eine Blinddarmentzündung [blint-darm-ent-ts*oo*n-g*oo*ng]
appetite der Appetit [–t*ee*t]
I've lost my appetite ich habe keinen Appetit mehr [ish hah-buh kine-en ... mair]
apple ein Apfel
application form das Antragsformular [–trahgs–]

10 APPOINTMENT

appointment ein Termin [tair-m*ee*n]
  may I make an appointment? könnte ich einen Termin ausmachen? [kurrntuh ish ine-en . . . ōwss-mah*k*en]
apricot eine Aprikose [app-ree-k*o*hzuh]
April April [appr*ee*l]
are sind [zinnt]
area die Gegend [gay-ghent]
  in the area in der Gegend
area code die Vorwahl [for-vahl]
arm der Arm
around: is he around? ist er da? [. . . air . . .]
arrange: will you arrange it? können Sie das arrangieren? [kurrnen zee dass ar-ron-dj*ee*-ren]
  it's all arranged es ist alles arrangiert [ess ist al-ess ar-ron-dj*ee*rt]
arrest verhaften [fair-h*a*ff-ten]
  he's been arrested sie haben ihn verhaftet [zee hah-ben een . . .]
arrival die Ankunft [an-k∞nft]
arrive ankommen
  we only arrived yesterday wir sind erst gestern angekommen [veer zinnt airst ghess-tairn . . .]
art die Kunst [k∞nst]
art gallery die Kunstgalerie [k∞nst–]
arthritis die Arthritis [ar-tr*ee*-tiss]
artificial künstlich [k∞nstlish]
artist der Künstler [k∞nstler]
as: as quickly as you can so schnell Sie können [zoh shnell zee kurrnen]
  as much as you can so viel Sie können [. . . feel . . .]
  do as I do machen Sie es mir nach [mah*k*en zee ess meer nah*k*]
  as you like wie Sie wollen [vee zee vollen]
ashore an Land [an lannt]
ashtray ein Aschenbecher [ashen-besher]
ask fragen [frah-ghen]
  could you ask him to . . .? würden Sie ihn bitten, ob er . . .? [vōōrden zee een bit-en opp air]

that's not what I asked for das hab' ich nicht bestellt [dass hahb ish nisht buh-shtellt]
asleep: he's still asleep er schläft noch [air shlayft no*k*]
asparagus der Spargel [shpargel]
aspirin eine Schmerztablette [shmairts-tab-lettuh]
assistant der Assistent
asthma das Asthma [ast-mah]
at: at the airport am Flughafen
  at my hotel in meinem Hotel
  at one o'clock um ein Uhr [oom ine oor]
atmosphere die Atmosphäre [–f*a*y-ruh]
attitude die Einstellung [ine-shtell-oong]
attractive attraktiv [–t*ee*f]
  I think you're very attractive ich finde Sie sehr attraktiv [ish fin-duh zee zair . . .]
Aufzug elevator
August August [ōw-g*oo*st]
aunt: my aunt meine Tante [mine-uh tantuh]
Ausfahrt exit (highway)
Ausgang exit
Auskunft information
außer Betrieb out of order
Austria Österreich [urr-ster-rysh]
Austrian österreichisch [–ish]
  (person) Österreicher
  (woman) Österreicherin
Ausverkauf sale
ausverkauft sold out
authorities die Behörden [buh-h*u*rr-den]
automatic *(car)* der Automatik [ōw-t*o*h-m*a*h-tik]
away: go away! geh (weg)! [gay vek]
awful schrecklich [–lish]
axle die Achse [ak-suh]
baby ein Baby
  we'd like a baby-sitter wir brauchen einen Babysitter [veer brōw*k*en ine-en . . .]
baby-carrier die Baby-Tragetasche [–trah-guh-tash-uh]

12 BACK

back: I've got a bad back ich habe Schwierigkeiten mit meinem Rücken [ish hah-buh shvee-rish-kite-en mit mine-em rōōcken]
  I'll be right back ich bin bald wieder da [ish bin balt veeder dah]
  is he back? ist er wieder da?
  may I have my money back? kann ich mein Geld wiederhaben [kan ish mine gellt veeder-hah-ben]
  come back kommen Sie zurück! [. . . zee tsoo-rōōck]
  I go back tomorrow ich fahre morgen zurück [ish fah-ruh mor-ghen . . .]
  in back hinten
backpack der Rucksack [rōōck–]
bacon der Speck [shpeck]
  bacon and eggs Eier mit Speck [eye-er . . .]
bad schlecht [shlesht]
  not bad nicht schlecht
  too bad Pech! [pesh]
Bad bathroom
Baden verboten no swimming
bag die Tasche [tash-uh]
  (*suitcase*) der Koffer
  (*plastic*) die Tüte [tōō-tuh]
baggage das Gepäck [geh-peck]
  baggage check (*at station*) die Gepäckaufbewahrung [gheh-peck-ōwf-buh-vah-rōōng]
Bahnsteig platform
Bahnübergang grade crossing
baker der Bäcker [becker]
balcony der Balkon
  a room with a balcony ein Zimmer mit Balkon [ine tsimmer . . .]
ball der Ball [bal]
ball-point pen ein Kugelschreiber [koogel-shryber]
banana eine Banane [bananuh]
band (*music*) die Band [bannt]
  (*dance*) das Orchester [orkester]

BEACH 13

bandage die Binde [bin-duh]
  could you change the bandage? könnten Sie den Verband wechseln? [kurrnten zee dayn fair-bannt vek-seln]
Band-Aid adhesive bandage ein (Heft)pflaster [–pflass-ter]
bank die Bank
  » *TRAVEL TIP: banking hours normally Mon-Fri 8:30–1:00 & 2:30–4:00 with late hours Thursdays and sometimes Fridays closing 5:30; bank holidays see* **public**
bar die Bar
barber der (Herren)friseur [(. . .)free-zur]
bargain: it's a real bargain das ist wirklich günstig [dass isst virk-lish gōōn-stish]
barmaid die Bardame [bar-dam-uh]
barrette eine Haarspange [–shpang-uh]
bartender der Barkeeper
basket der Korb [korp]
bath das Bad [baht]
  may I take a bath? kann ich ein Bad nehmen? [kann ish ine baht nay-men]
  could you give me a bath towel? könnten Sie mir ein Badetuch geben? [kurrnten zee meer ine bah-duh-took gay-ben]
bathing suit der Badeanzug [bah-duh-ant-soog]
bathrobe der Bademantel [bah-duh–]
bathroom das Badezimmer [bah-duh-tsimmer]
  we want a room with a private bathroom wir hätten gerne ein Zimmer mit Bad [veer hetten gairn-uh ine tsimmer mit baht]
  may I use your bathroom? darf ich bitte mal Ihre Toilette benutzen? [darf ish bittuh mal ee-ruh twa-lettuh buh-nootsen]
battery die Batterie
be: to be sein [zine]
  don't be angry seien Sie nicht böse [zy-en zee nisht burr-zuh]
  be reasonable seien Sie vernünftig! [zy-en zee fair-nōōnftish]; *see* **he, she, I,** *etc.*
beach der Strand [shtrannt]

14 BEANS

beans die Bohnen [boh-nen]
beautiful schön [shurrn]
because weil [vile]
   because of the delay wegen der Verspätung [vayghen dair fair-spayt-oong]
bed ein Bett
   single bed/double bed ein Einzelbett/Doppelbett [... ine-tsel-bett ...]
   you haven't changed my bed Sie haben die Bettwäsche nicht gewechselt [zee hah-ben dee bett-vesh-uh nisht gheh-vek-selt]
   I'm going to bed ich geh' ins Bett [ish gay ints ...]
bedroom das Schlafzimmer [shlahf-tsimmer]
bee eine Biene [bee-nuh]
beef das Rindfleisch [rinnt-flysh]
beer ein Bier [beer]
   two beers, please zwei Bier, bitte [tsvy beer bittuh]
   YOU MAY THEN HEAR ...
   Pils oder Export? *Pils or Export?*
   (Pils is stronger)
   große oder kleine? *large or small? (large = 0.5 liter, small = 0.2)*
   eine Halbe = ½ *liter = 0.9 pints*
   eine Maß *typical in Bavaria = 1 liter; if you like a darker beer try 'ein Alt', though this is not available in all parts of Germany*
before: before breakfast vor dem Frühstück [for daym froo-shtook]
   before we leave bevor wir gehen [buh-for veer gay-en]
   I haven't been here before ich bin hier noch nie gewesen [ish bin heer nok nee gheh-vay-zen]
begin: when does it begin? wann fängt es an? [van fengt ...]
beginner der Anfänger [an-fenger]
beginner's slope der Idiotenhügel [id-ee-oh-ten-hoo-ghel]
behind hinter

BIG 15

Belgian belgisch [bel-ghish]
  (person) Belgier [bel-gheer]
  (woman) Belgierin
Belgium Belgien [bel-ghee-un]
believe: I don't believe you das glaub' ich Ihnen nicht [dass glōwp ish ee-nen nisht]
  I believe you ich glaub' Ihnen [ish glōwp ee-nen]
bell *(in hotel, etc.)* die Klingel
belong: that belongs to me das gehört mir [dass gheh-hurrt meer]
  who does this belong to? wem gehört das? [vaym gheh-hurrt dass]
below unter [ōonter]
belt der Gürtel [gūrtel]
berries die Beeren [bay-ren]
besetzt (rest room) occupied; (bus) full
beside neben [nay-ben]
best beste [best-uh]
  it's the best vacation I've ever had das ist mein schönster Urlaub [. . . mine shurrn-ster oor-lōwp]
Betreten verboten no trespassing
Betreten des Rasens verboten keep off the grass
better besser
  haven't you got anything better? haben Sie nichts Besseres? [hah-ben zee nix . . .]
  are you feeling better? geht es Ihnen besser? [gayt ess ee-nen besser]
  I'm feeling a lot better es geht mir viel besser [ess gayt meer feel besser]
between zwischen [tsvishen]
bewachter Parkplatz supervised parking lot
beyond über [ūber]
bicycle ein Fahrrad [fahr-raht]
big groß [grohss]
  a big one ein großer [ine grohss-er]
  that's too big das ist zu groß [. . . ist tsoo . . .]
  it's not big enough das ist nicht groß genug [dass ist nicht grohss gheh-noog]
  do you have a bigger one? haben Sie nichts Größeres? [hah-ben zee nix grurrss-er-es]

16 BIKINI

bikini ein Bikini
bill die Rechnung [resh-noong]
   may I have the bill, please? zahlen, bitte!
   [tsah-len bittuh]
billfold die Brieftasche [breef-tash-uh]
binding *(ski)* die Bindung [–oong]
bird der Vogel [foh-ghel]
birthday der Geburtstag [gheh-boorts-tahg]
   it's my birthday ich habe Geburtstag
   Happy Birthday Herzlichen Glückwunsch
   (zum Geburtstag)! [hairts-lishen glöock-voonsh
   tsoom gheh-boorts-tahg]
bit: just a bit nur ein bißchen [noor ine
   bis-shen]
   just a little bit for me nur ganz wenig für
   mich [noor gants vay-nish föor mish]
bite ein Biß [biss]
   (mosquito) ein Stich [stish]
bitte eintreten please enter
bitte klingeln please ring
bitte klopfen please knock
bitte nicht stören please do not disturb
bitter bitter
black schwarz [shvarts]
   he blacked out er ist ohnmächtig geworden
   [air ist ohn-mesh-tish gheh-vorden]
blanket die Decke [deck-uh]
   I'd like another blanket könnte ich noch eine
   Decke haben? [kurrntuh ish nok ine-uh deck-uh
   hah-ben]
bleach das Bleichmittel [blysh–]
bleed bluten [blooten]
bless you *(after sneeze)* Gesundheit! [gheh-
   zoont-hyte]
blind blind [blinnt]
   blind spot der tote Winkel
   [toh-tuh vinkel]
blister eine Blase [blah-zuh]
blocked *(pipe)* verstopft [fair-shtopft]
   (road) blockiert [block-eert]
blonde eine Blondine [blond-ee-nuh]
blood das Blut [bloot]

his blood type is ... er hat Blutgruppe ... [air hat bloot-groop-uh ...]
I have high blood pressure ich habe hohen Blutdruck [ish hah-buh hoh-en bloot-droock]
he needs a blood transfusion er braucht eine Bluttransfusion [air browkt ine-uh bloot-tranz-fooz-ee-ohn]
bloody Mary eine Bloody Mary
blouse die Bluse [bloo-zuh]
blue blau [blōw]
boarding house die Pension [pen-zee-ohn]
boarding pass die Bordkarte [bort-kartuh]
boat das Boot [boht]
  (bigger) das Schiff [shiff]
boat ride eine Bootsfahrt [bohts-fahrt]
body der Körper [kurrper]
  (dead body) eine Leiche [lysh-uh]
boil *(verb)* kochen [kok-en]
  (on skin) ein Furunkel [foor-oonkel]
boiled egg gekochtes Ei [geh-koktes eye]
bone der Knochen [kuh-noken]
  (fish) die Gräte [grayt-uh]
book das Buch [book]
bookstore eine Buchhandlung [book-hant-loong]
boot der Stiefel [shteefel]
booze der Alkohol
I had too much booze last night ich habe gestern abend zu viel getrunken [ish hah-buh ghestern ah-bent tsoo feel geh-troonken]
border die Grenze [grents-uh]
» *TRAVEL TIP: visa and minimum of one night stay needed for crossing into GDR; transit visa can be bought at border for non-stop car journeys to West Berlin*
bored: I'm bored mir ist langweilig [meer ist lang-vile-ish]
boring langweilig [lang-vile-ish]
born: I was born in ... ich bin in ... geboren [ish bin in ... geh-bor-ren]
  see **date**
boss der Chef

18 BOTH

both beide [by-duh]
  I'll take both of them ich nehme beide [ish nay-muh by-duh]
bottle die Flasche [flash-uh]
bottle opener der Flaschenöffner [flash-en-urrfner]
bottom: at the bottom of the... unten am... [oonten...]
bouncer der Rausschmeißer [rowss-shmysser]
bowl *(basin)* die Schüssel [shoossel]
box die Schachtel [shahktel]
  (wood) die Kiste [kistuh]
box office die Kasse [kassuh]
boy ein Junge [yoonguh]
boyfriend der Freund [froynt]
bra der BH [bay-hah]
bracelet das Armband [–bannt]
brake die Bremse [brem-zuh]
  could you check the brakes? könnten Sie die Bremsen nachsehen? [kurrnten zee dee brem-zen nahk-zay-en]
  I had to brake suddenly ich mußte plötzlich bremsen [ish moostuh plurrts-lish brem-zen]
  he didn't brake er hat nicht gebremst [air hat nisht geh-bremst]
brandy der Weinbrand [vine-brannt]
bread das Brot [broht]
  could we have some bread and butter? könnten wir etwas Brot und Butter haben? [kurrnten veer etvass broht oont booter hah-ben]
  some more bread, please noch etwas Brot, bitte [nok etvass broht bittuh]
break brechen [breshen]
  I think I've broken my arm ich glaube, ich habe mir den Arm gebrochen [... glowbuh ish hah-buh meer ... geh-broken]
  my car broke down mein Wagen ist stehengeblieben [mine vah-ghen ist shtay-en-gheh-bleeben]
breakdown die Panne [pan-uh]
» *TRAVEL TIP: highway patrols give free help*

BROWSE 19

(except parts); telephone for 'Straßenwachthilfe' [shtrahss-en-vah*k*t-hilfuh]
nervous breakdown Nervenzusammenbruch [nairven-tsoo-zammen-bro͞o*k*]
breakfast das Frühstück [fro͞o-sto͞ock]
 full/Continental breakfast englisches/kleines Frühstück [... kline-es ...]
breast die Brust [bro͞ost]
breath der Atem [ah-tem]
breathe atmen [aht-men]
 I can't breathe ich bekomme keine Luft [ish buh-kommuh kine-uh lo͞oft]
bridge die Brücke [bro͞ockuh]
briefcase die (Akten)mappe [(...)mappuh]
briefs die Unterhose [o͞onter-hoh-zuh]
brilliant *(very good)* großartig [grohss-ahrtish]
bring bringen
 could you bring it to my hotel? könnten Sie es mir ins Hotel bringen? [kurrnten zee ess meer ints ...]
Britain Großbritannien [grohss-bri-t*a*hn-ee-un]
British britisch [bree-tish]
 the British die Briten [bree-ten]
brochure der Prospekt
 do you have any brochures on ...? haben Sie Prospekte über ...? [hah-ben zee ... o͞ober]
broke: I'm broke ich bin pleite [ish bin ply-tuh]
broken kaputt
 you've broken it Sie haben es kaputt gemacht [zee hah-ben ess ... geh-m*a*h*k*t]
 my room/car has been broken into man ist in mein Zimmer eingebrochen/man hat meinen Wagen aufgebrochen [... mine tsimmer ine-geh-bro*k*en/... mine-en vah-ghen o͞owf-gheh-bro*k*en]
brooch die Brosche [broh-shuh]
brother: my brother mein Bruder [mine brooder]
brown braun [brōwn]
browse: may I just browse around? kann ich mich mal umsehen? [kan ish mish mal o͞om-zay-en]

20 BRUISE

bruise ein blauer Fleck [ine blow-er ...]
brunette eine Brünette [ine-uh broo-nettuh]
brush die Bürste [boorstuh]
  (artist's) der Pinsel
Brussels sprouts der Rosenkohl [roh-zen-kohl]
bucket der Eimer [eye-mer]
buffet das Büffet [boof-ay]
building das Gebäude [gheh-boy-duh]
bulb die (Glüh)birne [(gloo)beern-uh]
  the bulb is burned out die Birne ist durchgebrannt [... ist doorsh-gheh-brannt]
bump: he's had a bump on the head er hat sich den Kopf angeschlagen [air hat zish dayn kopf an-gheh-shlah-ghen]
bumper die Stoßstange [shtohss-shtang-uh]
bunch of flowers ein Blumenstrauß [bloomen-shtrōwss]
bunk das Bett; *(in ship)* die Koje [koh-yuh]
  bunk beds ein Etagenbett [ay-tahj-en–]
buoy die Boje [boh-yuh]
burglar ein Einbrecher [ine-breker]
  they've taken all my money man hat mir mein ganzes Geld gestohlen [... meer mine gants-es gelt gheh-shtohlen]
burnt: this meat is burnt das Fleisch ist angebrannt [flysh ist an-gheh-brannt]
  my arms are burnt ich habe Sonnenbrand an den Armen [ish hah-buh zonnen-brannt]
  can you give me something for these burns? können Sie mir etwas für diese Brandwunden geben? [kurrnen zee meer etvass foor deez-uh brannt-voonden gay-ben]
bus der Bus [booss]
  bus stop die Bushaltestelle [booss-haltuh-shtelluh]
  could you tell me when we get there? können Sie mir sagen, wo ich aussteigen muß? [kurrnen zee meer zah-ghen voh ish ōwss-shty-ghen mooss]

» *TRAVEL TIP: on town bus routes you may have to buy your ticket from a machine near the bus stop before you get on the bus*

business das Geschäft [gheh-sheft]
   I'm here on business ich bin geschäftlich hier [ish bin gheh-sheft-lish heer]
   business trip eine Geschäftsreise [ine-uh gheh-shefts-ry-zuh]
   that's none of your business das geht Sie nichts an [dass gayt zee nix an]
bust die Büste [boostuh]
   (measurement) die Oberweite [ohber-vy-tuh]
» *TRAVEL TIP: bust measurements*
   US   32   34   36   38   40
   Germany 80 87 91 97 102
busy beschäftigt [buh-sheft-isht]
   (telephone) besetzt
   are you busy? haben Sie viel zu tun? [hah-ben zee feel tsoo toon]
but aber [ah-ber]
   not...but... nicht...sondern...[nisht...zondern]
butcher der Fleischer [flysher]
butter die Butter [booter]
button der Knopf [kuh-nopf]
buy kaufen [kowfen]
   where can I buy...? wo kann ich...kaufen? [voh...]
   I'll buy it ich nehme es [ish nay-muh ess]
by: I'm here by myself ich bin allein hier [ish bin al-ine heer]
   can you do it by tomorrow? können Sie es bis morgen erledigen? [kurrnen zee...air-layd-i-ghen]
   by train/car/plane per Zug/Auto/Flugzeug [pair...]
   I parked by the trees ich habe bei den Bäumen geparkt [ish hah-buh by dayn boy-men gheh-parkt]
   who's it made by? wer ist der Hersteller? [vair ist dair hair-shteller]
cabaret das Variété [vah-ree-ay-tay]
cabaret show das Kabarett [kabah-ray]
cabbage der Kohl
cable das Kabel [kah-bel]

22 CABLE CAR

cable car die Seilbahn [zyle-bahn]
cabin *(on ship)* die Kabine [kabeen-uh]
cafe ein Café
» *TRAVEL TIP: in the 'Konditorei' or 'Café' you will get mostly coffee and pastries; alcohol and snacks are served too; for a fuller meal go to an 'Imbißstube' or 'Schnellimbiß'; otherwise a 'Wirtschaft' or 'Lokal'*
cake der Kuchen [kooken]
  a piece of cake ein Stück Kuchen [ine shtōōck kooken]
calculator der Taschenrechner [tashen-reshner]
call: will you call the manager? rufen Sie den Geschäftsführer, bitte! [roofen zee dayn geh-sheftss-fōōrer bittuh]
  what is this called? wie nennt man das?
calm ruhig [roo-ish]
  calm down beruhigen Sie sich! [buh-roo-ig-en zee zish]
camera die Kamera
camp: can we camp here? können wir hier zelten? [kurrnen veer heer tselten]
  camping vacation ein Camping-Urlaub [... oor-lōwp]
camper *(vehicle)* der Wohnmobil [vohn-moh-beel]
campsite der Campingplatz
» *TRAVEL TIP: off-site camping requires permission of land-owner and/or local police*
can¹: a can of beer eine Dose Bier [ine-uh doh-zuh beer]
can²: can I have...? kann ich... haben? [kan ish ... hah-ben]
  can you...? können Sie... [kurrnen zee]
  I can't... ich kann nicht... [ish kan nisht]
  he can't... er kann nicht... [air ...]
  we can't... wir können nicht... [veer ...]
Canada Kanada
Canadian kanadisch
  (person) Kanadier [kanah-deer]
  (woman) Kanadierin

CASSETTE 23

cancel: **I want to cancel my reservation** ich möchte meine Buchung rückgängig machen [ish murrshtuh mine-uh boo*k*-oong r*oo*ck-geng-ish ˈmah*k*en]
 can we cancel dinner for tonight? können wir das Abendessen für heute abbestellen? [kurrnen veer dass ah-bent-essen f*oo*r hoy-tuh app-buh-shtellen]
candle die Kerze [kairts-uh]
candy Süßigkeiten [z*oo*ss-ish-kite-en]
 a piece of candy ein Bonbon
can opener ein Dosenöffner [doh-zen-urrfner]
car das Auto, der Wagen [*ow*-toh, vah-ghen]
carafe die Karaffe [kar-*a*ffuh]
carbonated *(drink)* mit Kohlensäure [mit kohlen-zoy-ruh]
carburetor der Vergaser [fair-g*a*hzer]
card die Karte
 do you play cards? spielen Sie Karten? [shpeelen zee . . .]
care: **will you take care of my briefcase for me?** würden Sie auf meine Aktenmappe aufpassen? [v*oo*rden zee *o*wf mine-uh akten-mappuh *o*wf-pas-en]
 goodbye, take care mach's gut [mah*k*s goot]
careful: **be careful** seien Sie vorsichtig [zy-en zee f*o*r-zish-tish]
carpet der Teppich [teppish]
carrot eine Karotte [karottuh]
carry: **will you carry this for me?** könnten Sie dies für mich tragen? [kurrnten zee deess f*oo*r mish trah-ghen]
carving die Schnitzerei [shnits-er-*eye*]
cash das Bargeld [bar-gelt]
 I don't have any cash ich habe es nicht in bar [ish hah-buh es nisht in bar]
 will you cash a check for me? können Sie mir einen Scheck einlösen? [kurrnen zee meer ine-en sheck ine-lurrzen]
cash register die Kasse [kassuh]
casino das Kasino
cassette eine Cassette [kassett-uh]

24 CASSETTE RECORDER

cassette recorder ein Cassettenrekorder
castle das Schloß [schloss]
  (fortress) die Burg
cat eine Katze [kats-uh]
catch: where do we catch the bus? wo fährt der Bus ab? [voh fairt dair booss app]
  he's caught a bug er hat sich irgendwo angesteckt [air hat zish irgend-voh an-gheh-shteckt]
cathedral die Kathedrale [kah-tay-drahl-uh]
Catholic katholisch [kah-toh-lish]
cauliflower der Blumenkohl [bloomen-kohl]
cave die Höhle [hurr-luh]
ceiling die Decke [deck-uh]
celery der Stangensellerie [shtang-en-zeller-ee]
cellophane das Cellophan [tsello-fahn]
center das Zentrum [tsen-troom]
  how do we get to the center of town? wie kommen wir zur Stadtmitte? [vee kommen veer tsoor shtatt-mittuh]
centigrade Celsius [tsel-zee-ooss]
» *TRAVEL TIP: to convert C to F:* $\frac{C}{5} \times 9 + 32 = F$

centigrade	−10	−5	0	10	15	21	30	36.9
Fahrenheit	14	23	32	50	59	70	86	98.4

centimeter ein Zentimeter [tsentee-may-ter]
» *TRAVEL TIP: 1 cm = 0.39 inches*
central zentral [tsen-trahl]
  with central heating mit Zentralheizung [mit tsen-trahl-hyts-oong]
certain bestimmt [buh-shtimmt]
  are you certain? sind Sie sicher? [zinnt zee zisher]
certificate eine Bescheinigung [buh-shine-ee-goong]
chain die Kette [kettuh]
chair der Stuhl [shtool]
  (armchair) der Sessel [zessel]
chairlift der Sessellift
champagne der Sekt [zekt]

CHECK 25

change: could you change this into marks?
könnten Sie das in Mark umtauschen?
[kurrnten zee dass ... oom-tōw-shen]
I don't have any change ich habe kein
Kleingeld [ish hah-buh kine kline-gelt]
do we have to change trains? müssen wir
umsteigen? [mōōssen veer oom-shtigh-ghen]
I'll have to get changed ich muß mich
umziehen [ish mooss mish oom-tsee-en]
**I'd like to change my reservation/flight
etc** ich möchte umbuchen [ish murrshtuh
oom-book*en*]
channel: the English Channel der
Ärmelkanal [airmel-kan*a*l]
charge: what do you charge? was verlangen
Sie? [vass fair-l*a*ngen zee]
who's in charge? wer hat hier die Verantwortung? [vair hat heer dee fair-*a*nt-vort-oong]
chart *(flow chart, etc.)* das Diagramm
[dee-ah-gr*a*hm]
cheap billig [bi*l*lish]
something cheaper etwas Billigeres [etvass
billig-er-es]
cheat: I've been cheated ich bin betrogen
worden [ish bin buh-tr*o*h-ghen vorden]
check¹ der Scheck [sheck]
will you take a check? nehmen Sie
Schecks? [nay-men zee shecks]
checkbook das Scheckbuch [sheck-boo*k*]
check²: will you check? sehen Sie bitte nach
[zay-en zee bittuh nah*k*]
I've checked ich habe nachgeprüft [ish
hah-buh nah*k*-gheh-pr*ōō*ft]
will you check the total? könnten Sie das
nachrechnen? [kurrnten zee das
n*a*hk-resh-nen]
we checked in/we checked out wir haben
uns angemeldet/abgemeldet [veer hah-ben
oonts angheh-meldet/app-gheh-meldet]
check³ die Rechnung
may I have the check please? zahlen, bitte
[tsah-len bittuh]

26 CHECKROOM

checkroom die Garderobe [garduh-robe-uh]
cheek die Backe [back-uh]
cheers *(toast)* Prost [prohst]
cheese der Käse [kay-zuh]
   say cheese bitte recht freundlich [bittuh resht froynt-lish]
cheesecake der Käsekuchen [–kooken]
chef der Koch [kok]
chest die Brust [broost]
» *TRAVEL TIP: chest measurements*

US	34	36	38	40	42	44	46
Germany	87	91	97	102	107	112	117

chewing gum der Kaugummi [kow-goomee]
chicken ein Hähnchen [hayn-shen]
chicken pox die Windpocken [vintpocken]
child ein Kind [kint]
   children die Kinder [kinder]
   children's portion ein Kinderteller
» *TRAVEL TIP: no law against taking children into a bar*
chin das Kinn
china das Porzellan [ports-ellan]
chips *(to eat, in casino)* die Chips
chocolate die Schokolade [shok-oh-lahduh]
   hot chocolate (heiße) Schokolade [hyssuh]
   a box of chocolates Pralinen [prah-leenen]
choke *(car)* der Choke
chop ein Kotelett [kot-lett]
   pork/lamb chop Schweine-/Lammkotelett
Christmas Weihnachten [vy-nahk-ten]
   Merry Christmas fröhliche Weihnachten [frurrlish-uh ...]
   Christmas Eve Heiligabend [hile-ish-ahbent]
» *TRAVEL TIP: Christmas in Germany starts on the 24th (Heiligabend) when work normally stops at midday; presents are given on the evening of the 24th; holidays on Christmas Day (der erste Weihnachtstag) and the day after Christmas (der zweite Weihnachtstag); on December 6 children find candy and nuts left in their shoes during the night by St. Nikolaus*
church die Kirche [keer-shuh]

CLOTH 27

where is the Protestant/Catholic church?
wo ist die evangelische/katholische Kirche?
[voh ist dee . . .]
cider der Apfelmost
cigar die Zigarre [tsigarruh]
cigarette die Zigarette [tsigarr-ettuh]
 would you like a cigarette? darf ich Ihnen eine Zigarette anbieten? [. . . ish een-en ine-uh tsigarr-ettuh an-bee-ten]
city die Stadt [shtatt]
claim *(insurance)* der Anspruch [an-shprook]
clarify klären [klairen]
clean *(adjective)* sauber [zōwber]
 may I have some clean sheets? kann ich frische Bettwäsche haben? [kan ish frish-uh bett-vesh-uh hah-ben]
 my room hasn't been cleaned today in meinem Zimmer ist heute nicht saubergemacht worden [in mine-em tsimmer ist hoy-tuh nisht zōwber-gheh-mahkt vorden]
 it's not clean das ist nicht sauber
clear klar
 it's not clear to me ich bin mir darüber nicht im klaren [ish bin meer darōober nisht . . .]
 do you think it will clear up later? glauben Sie, es klärt sich später auf? [glōwben zee ess klairt zish shpayter ōwf]
clever klug [kloog]
 (skillful) geschickt [gheh-shickt]
climate das Klima [klee-mah]
climb: we're going to climb . . . wir besteigen . . . [veer buh-shty-ghen]
climber ein Bergsteiger [bairk-shty-gher]
climbing boots die Bergstiefel [bairk-shteefel]
clip *(ski: on boot)* die Schnalle [shnall-uh]
clock die Uhr [oor]
close[1] *(adverb)* nahe [nah-uh]
close[2]**: when do you close?** wann machen Sie zu? [van mahken zee tsoo]
closed geschlossen [gheh-shlossen]
closet der Schrank [shrank]
cloth das Tuch [took]

28 CLOTHES

clothes die Kleidung [kly-doong]
clothespin die Wäscheklammer [vesh-uh–]
cloud die Wolke [vol-kuh]
clutch *(car)* die Kupplung [koop-loong]
  the clutch is slipping die Kupplung schleift [... shlyft]
coast die Küste [koostuh]
coast guard die Küstenwache [koosten-vahk-uh]
coat der Mantel; *(of suit)* das Jackett [yackett]
cockroach eine Küchenschabe [kooken-shah-buh]
coffee ein Kaffee [kaffay]
  coffee with milk/black coffee Kaffee mit Milch/Kaffee schwarz [... mit milsh/ ... shvarts]
  two coffees, please zwei Kaffee, bitte [tsvy kaffay bittuh]
  YOU MAY THEN HEAR ...
  Kännchen oder Tassen? *pots or cups? a pot is usually 2 cups; bring your own artificial sweeteners*
coin die Münze [moon-tsuh]
cold kalt
  I'm cold ich friere [ish free-ruh]
  I have a cold ich bin erkältet [ish bin air-keltet]
cold cream die Reinigungscreme [rine-ee-goongs-kray-muh]
collapse: he's collapsed er ist zusammengebrochen [air ist tsoo-zammen-gheh-broken]
collar der Kragen [krah-ghen]
» *TRAVEL TIP: continental sizes*
  US: 14   14½   15   15½   16   16½   17
  Germany: 36   37   38   39   41   42   43
collarbone das Schlüsselbein [shloossel-bine]
collect call ein R-Gespräch [air-gheh-shpraysh]
  I want to make a collect call to Dallas ich möchte ein R-Gespräch nach Dallas anmelden [ish murrshtuh ...]
» *TRAVEL TIP: collect calls are not possible within Germany*

collision der Zusammenstoß
[tsoo-*za*mmen-shtohss]
color die Farbe [far-buh]
  have you any other colors? haben Sie noch
andere Farben? [hah-ben zee no*k* ander-uh
far-ben]
comb ein Kamm
come kommen
  I come from Chicago ich komme aus Chicago
[ish kommuh ōwss . . .]
  we came here yesterday wir sind gestern
hier angekommen [veer zinnt ghestern heer
an-gheh-kommen]
  when is he coming? wann kommt er? [van
kommt air]
  come in herein! [hair-rine]
  come on! komm!
  come with me kommen Sie mit! [. . . zee . . .]
comfortable bequem [buh-kv*a*ym]
  it's not very comfortable es ist nicht sehr
bequem [. . . nisht zayr buh-kv*a*ym]
company die Gesellschaft [gheh-*ze*ll-shafft]
  you're good company ich bin gern mit Ihnen
zusammen [ish bin gairn mit ee-nen
tsoo-*za*mmen]
compartment *(train)* das Abteil [app-tile]
compass der Kompaß [kom-pas]
compensation die Entschädigung
[ent-sh*a*yd-ee-g*oo*ng]
  I demand compensation ich verlange
Schadenersatz [ish fair-l*a*ng-uh
shaden-airsats]
complain sich beschweren [zish buh-shv*ai*ren]
  I want to complain about the waiter ich
möchte mich über den Kellner beschweren [ish
murrshtuh mish ōōber dayn kellner . . .]
completely völlig [furrlish]
complicated: it's very complicated es ist sehr
kompliziert [. . . zair komplits-*ee*rt]
compliment das Kompliment [–m*e*nt]
  my compliments to the chef ein Lob der
Küche [ine lohp dair k*ōō*k-uh]

30 CONCERT

concert das Konzert [kont*ai*rt]
concussion eine Gehirnerschütterung [gheh-h*i*rn-air-shoot-eroong]
condition die Bedingung [buh-d*i*ng-oong]
   it's not in very good condition es ist nicht in besonders gutem Zustand [... nisht in buh-z*o*nders gootem tsoo-shtant]
condom ein Kondom [kon-d*o*hm]
conference die Konferenz [kon-fer-*e*nts]
confession das Geständnis [gheh-sht*e*nt-nis]
confirm bestätigen [buh-st*a*yt-ee-goong]
confuse: you're confusing me Sie bringen mich durcheinander [zee bringen mish d*oo*rsh-ine-ander]
congratulations! herzlichen Glückwunsch! [hairts-lishen gloock-voonsh]
con-man der Schwindler [shv*i*ntler]
connection die Verbindung [fair-b*i*n-doong]
connoisseur der Kenner
conscious bewußt [buh-v*oo*st]
consciousness: he's lost consciousness er ist bewußtlos [air ist buh-v*oo*st-lohs]
constipation die Verstopfung [fair-sht*o*pf-oong]
consul der Konsul [kon-z*oo*l]
consulate das Konsulat [kon-zool-*a*ht]
contact: how can I contact ...? wie kann ich ... erreichen? [vee kan ish ... air-r*y*shen]
   I'll get in contact soon ich werde mich melden [ish vairduh mish ...]
contact lenses die Kontaktlinsen [–zen]
contraceptive ein empfängnisverhütendes Mittel [emp-feng-nis-fair-hoot-end-ess ...]
convenient günstig [goonstish]
cook: it's not cooked es ist nicht gar
   you're a good cook Sie kochen ausgezeichnet [zee koken ōwss-gheh-tsysh-net]
cookie ein Plätzchen [plets-shen]
cool kühl [kōōl]
corkscrew der Korkenzieher [–tsee-er]
corn *(foot)* ein Hühnerauge [hōōner-ōwg-uh]
corner die Ecke [eck-uh]

may we have a corner table? können wir einen Ecktisch haben? [kurrnen veer ine-en eck-tish hah-ben]
cornflakes die Cornflakes
corn on the cob der Maiskolben [mice-kolben]
correct richtig [rish-tish]
cosmetics die Kosmetika [kosmaytikah]
cost: what does it cost? was kostet das? [vass kostet dass]
   that's too much das ist zu viel [dass ist tsoo feel]
   I'll take it ich nehme es [ish nay-muh ess]
cotton die Baumwolle [bōwm-volluh]
cough der Husten [hoosten]
   cough drops die Hustentropfen
   cough medicine der Hustensaft [–zaft]
could: could you please . . . könnten Sie, bitte, . . .? [kurrnten zee bittuh . . .]
   could I have . . .? dürfte ich . . . haben? [dōōrf-tuh ish . . . hah-ben]
   we couldn't . . . wir konnten nicht . . . [veer]
country das Land [lannt]
   in the country auf dem Land [ōwf daym lannt]
couple: a couple of . . . ein paar . . . [ine pahr]
course *(of meal)* der Gang
   of course natürlich [natōōr-lish]
court: I'll take you to court ich werde Sie vor Gericht bringen [ish vair-duh zee for gheh-risht . . .]
cousin der Cousin; die Cousine [koo-zan koo-zeen-uh]
cover: cover him up decken Sie ihn zu [. . . zee een tsoo]
cover charge ein Gedeck [gheh-deck]
crab die Krabbe [krabbuh]
cracker ein Kräker [krecker]
crazy verrückt [fair-rōōckt]
   you're crazy du spinnst [doo shpinnst]
cream die Sahne [zah-nuh]
   (with butter) die Creme [kray-muh]
   (for skin) die Creme
   (color) cremefarben [–far-ben]

32 CREDIT CARD

credit card die Kreditkarte [kred*ee*t-kartuh]
crisis die Krise [kree-zuh]
crossroads die Kreuzung [kroytsoong]
crosswalk der Fußgängerüberweg
 [fooss-genger-oober-vayg]
» *TRAVEL TIP: be warned, the Germans take the red
 light for pedestrians seriously; you can be fined
 on the spot for crossing against the light*
crowded überfüllt [oober-foolt]
crutch die Krücke [krook-uh]
cry: don't cry weinen Sie nicht [vine-en zee
 nisht]
cup die Tasse [ta*ss*-uh]
 a cup of coffee eine Tasse Kaffee [ine-uh
 tass-uh kaffay]
cupboard der Schrank [shrank]
curry der Curry
curtains der Vorhang [for-hang]
curve die Kurve [koor-vuh]
cushion das Kissen
Customs der Zoll [tsoll]
cut: I've cut myself ich habe mich geschnitten
 [ish hah-buh mish gheh-shni*tt*en]
cylinder der Zylinder [tsoo*li*nder]
 cylinder head gasket die Zylinderkopf-
 dichtung [tsoolinder-kopf-dish-toong]
damage: I'll pay for the damage ich werde für
 den Schaden aufkommen [ish vair-duh foor
 dayn shahden owf-kommen]
 it's damaged es ist beschädigt [es ist
 buh-sha*y*d-isht]
Damen Ladies' rest room
damn! verdammt! [fair-da*mm*t]
damp feucht [foysht]
dance der Tanz
 would you like to dance? möchten Sie
 tanzen? [murrshten zee tantsen]
dangerous gefährlich [gheh-fa*i*r-lish]
dark dunkel [doonkel]
 when does it get dark? wann wird es dunkel?
 [van veert ess doonkel]
 dark blue dunkelblau [doonkel-blow]

DELAY 33

darling Liebling [leep-ling]
dashboard das Armaturenbrett [–tooren–]
date: what's the date der wievielte ist heute?
  [dair vee-feel-tuh ist hoy-tuh]
  can we set a date? können wir einen Termin
  ausmachen? [kurrnen veer ine-en tair-meen
  ōwss-mahken]
  on May 5 am fünften Mai [am fōōnften my]
  in 1951 neunzehnhunderteinundfünfzig
  [noyn-tsayn-hoondert-ine-oont-fōōnf-tsish]
» *TRAVEL TIP: to say the date in German, add letters
'ten' to the number if 1–19, and 'sten' if 20–31;
see numbers on p. 128; exceptions:* **first** *ersten;*
third *dritten;* **seventh** *siebten; when writing
the date in figures, Europeans put the day before
the month; so European 8/1/84 is equivalent to
our 1/8/84*
daughter: my daughter meine Tochter
  [mine-uh tokter]
day der Tag [tahg]
Deutsche Demokratische Republik, DDR *East
Germany, GDR*
dead tot [toht]
deaf taub [tōwp]
deal *(business)* das Geschäft [gheh-sheft]
  it's a deal abgemacht [app-gheh-mahkt]
dear:
  Dear Mr. Kunz Sehr geehrter Herr Kunz
  Dear Franz Lieber Franz
  Dear Sir *if no name known write:* Sehr geehrte
  Damen und Herren
December Dezember [dayts–]
deck das Deck
deck chair der Liegestuhl [leeguh-shtool]
declare: nothing to declare nichts zu
  verzollen [nix tsoo fair-tsollen]
deep tief [teef]
defendant der Angeklagte [an-gheh-klahg-tuh]
  (in civil cases) der Beklagte [buh–]
de-icer spray der Enteiser [ent-eyes-er]
delay: the flight was delayed der Flug hatte
  Verspätung [dair floog hat-uh fair-shpayt-oong]

34 DELIBERATELY

deliberately absichtlich [app-zisht-lish]
delicate *(person)* zart [tsart]
delicatessen ein Delikatessengeschäft [–gheh-sheft]
delicious köstlich [kurrst-lish]
delivery die Lieferung [leeferoong]
  is there another mail delivery? gibt es noch eine Zustellung? [gheept ess nok ine-uh tsoo-shtel-oong]
deluxe Luxus– [looxooss]
democratic demokratisch [–krah-tish]
demonstration *(of gadget)* eine Vorführung [for-foor-roong]
Denmark Dänemark [day-nuh-mark]
dent die Delle [delluh]
  you've dented my car Sie haben eine Delle in mein Auto gefahren [zee hah-ben ine-uh del-uh in mine ōw-toh gheh-fah-ren]
dentist der Zahnarzt [tsahn-artst]
  YOU MAY HEAR ...
  bitte weit öffnen *open wide*
  bitte ausspülen *rinse out*
  Sie brauchen drei Füllungen *you need three fillings*
  möchten Sie eine Spritze? *would you like an injection?*
dentures das Gebiß [gheh-biss]
  (partial) die Zahnprothese [tsahn-proh-tay-zuh]
deny: I deny it das bestreite ich [dass buh-shtry-tuh ish]
deodorant das Deodorant [day–]
departure die Abreise [app-ry-zuh]
  (bus, train) die Abfahrt
  (plane) der Abflug [app-floog]
depend: it depends das kommt darauf an [... da-rōwf ...]
  it depends on him das kommt auf ihn an
deposit die Anzahlung [antsah-loong]
  do I have to leave a deposit? muß ich eine Kaution hinterlegen? [mooss ish ine-uh kōw-tsee-ohn hinterlay-ghen]

DIFFICULT 35

depressed deprimiert [day-prim-*ee*rt]
desperate: I'm desperate for a drink ich brauche dringend was zu trinken [ish brōw*k*uh dringent ... tsoo ...]
dessert der Nachtisch [nah*k*–]
destination das Reiseziel [ry-zuh-tseel]
(of goods) der Bestimmungsort [buh-sht*i*m-œngs-ort]
detergent das Waschmittel
laundry detergent das Waschpulver [vash-pœlver]
detour der Umweg [œm-vayg]
devalued abgewertet [app-gheh-vairtet]
develop: could you develop these? könnten Sie diese entwickeln? [kurrnten zee dee-zuh ent-v–]
diabetic ein Diabetiker [dee–]
(woman) eine Diabetikerin
(adjective) diabetisch [dee-ah-b*a*y-tish]
diamond der Diamant [dee–]
diaper die Windel [v*i*ndel]
diaphragm cream Diaphragmacreme [dee-ah-fr*a*g-ma-kraymuh]
diarrhea der Durchfall [d*œ*rsh-fal]
have you got something for diarrhea? haben Sie ein Mittel gegen Durchfall? [hah-ben zee ...]
diary das Tagebuch [tah-gheh-boo*k*]
dictionary ein Wörterbuch [vurr-ter-boo*k*]
die sterben [shtairben]
he's dying er stirbt [air shteerbt]
diesel *(fuel)* Diesel
diet die Diät [dee-*a*yt]
I'm on a diet ich mache eine Schlankheitskur [ish mah*k*-uh ine-uh shlank-hites-koor]
different: they are different sie sind verschieden [zee zinnt fair-sh*ee*-den]
may I have a different room? kann ich ein anderes Zimmer haben? [... ine an-der-es ...]
is there a different route? gibt es eine andere Strecke?
difficult schwierig [shveerish]

36 DIGESTION

digestion die Verdauung [fair-dōw-ɶng]
dinghy das Ding(h)i
  (collapsible) das Schlauchboot [shlōwk-boht]
dining car *(rail)* der Speisewagen
  [shpyzuh-vah-ghen]
dining room das Eßzimmer [ess-tsimmer]
  (in hotel) der Speiseraum [shpy-zuh-rōwm]
dinner das (Abend)essen [ah-bent-]
dinner jacket die Smokingjacke [–yackuh]
direct *(adjective)* direkt [dee–]
  does it go direct? ist es eine Direkt-
  verbindung? [... ine-uh deerekt-fairbindɶng]
dirty schmutzig [shmɶtsish]
disabled behindert [buh-hinndert]
disappear verschwinden [fair-shvinnden]
  it just disappeared es ist einfach
  verschwunden [ess ist ine-fahk fair-shvɶnden]
disappointing enttäuschend [ent-toyshent]
disco die Disko
discount der Rabatt
  cash discount Skonto
disgusting widerlich [veeder-lish]
dish *(food)* das Gericht [geh-risht]
  (plate) die Schüssel [shɶssel]
dishwashing liquid das Spülmittel
  [shpōōl-mittel]
dishonest unehrlich [ɶn-airlish]
disinfectant das Desinfektionsmittel
  [days-infek-tsee-ohns-]
distance die Entfernung [ent-fair-nɶng]
  in the distance in der Ferne
  [in dair fairnuh]
distress signal ein Notsignal [noht-zignahl]
distributor *(car)* der Verteiler [fair-tyler]
disturb: the noise is disturbing us der Lärm
  stört uns [dair lairm shturrt ɶnts]
divorced geschieden [geh-sheeden]
do machen [mahken]
  how do you do? guten Tag [gooten tahg]
  (in the evening) guten Abend [gooten ah-bent]
  what are you doing tonight? was machen
  Sie heute abend? [vass ... zee hoytuh ah-bent]

DRESS 37

how do you do it? wie machen Sie das? [vee ... zee ...]
will you do it for me? machen Sie das für mich? [... foor mish]
I've never done it before ich habe das noch nie gemacht [ish hah-buh dass no*k* nee geh-m*ah*kt]
he did it das hat er gemacht [... air geh-m*ah*kt]
I was doing 60 kph ich fuhr mit 60 km/h [ish foor mit zesh-tsish]
doctor der Arzt
I need a doctor ich brauche einen Arzt [ish br*oo*k uh ine-en ...]
YOU MAY HEAR...
haben Sie das schon einmal gehabt? *have you had this before?*
wo tut es weh? *where does it hurt?*
nehmen Sie zur Zeit Medikamente? *are you taking any drugs at the moment?*
nehmen Sie eine davon dreimal/viermal täglich *take one of these three/four times a day*
document das Dokument [–ooment]
dog ein Hund [h*oo*nt]
dollar der Dollar
don't! nicht! [nisht] *see* **not**
door die Tür [t*oo*r]
doorman der Hotelboy
dosage die Dosis [doh-ziss]
double: double room Doppelzimmer [–tsimmer]
double scotch ein doppelter Whisky
down: get down! runter! [r*oo*nter]
it's down the road es ist nur ein Stückchen weiter [... noor ine shtook-shen vy-ter]
he's downstairs er ist unten [... *oo*nten]
drain das (Abfluß)rohr [app-fl*oo*ss-ror]
dress das Kleid [klite]
» TRAVEL TIP: *dress sizes*

US	6	8	10	12	14	16	18
Germany	36	38	40	42	44	46	48

38 DRESSING

dressing *(for wound)* der Verband [fair-bannt]
(for salad) die Sauce [zohsuh]
drink: would you like a drink? möchten Sie etwas trinken? [murrshten zee etvass...]
I don't drink ich trinke keinen Alkohol [ish trinkuh kine-en al-koh-hohl]
is the water drinkable? kann man das Wasser trinken?
drive fahren
I've been driving all day ich bin den ganzen Tag gefahren [ish... gantsen tahg gheh–]
» *TRAVEL TIP: driving in Germany – speed limits: 50 kph (31 mph) in town; 100 (62) outside; highways 130 (81) recommended with 60 (37) minimum; trucks and trailers max. 80 (49); seat belt, emergency red triangle (distress signal) and first aid kit compulsory*
driver der Fahrer
driver's license der Führerschein [foorer-shine]
drown: he's drowning er ertrinkt [air airtrinkt]
drücken push
drug das Medikament
(marijuana, etc.) die Droge [droh-ghuh]
drugstore eine Drogerie [droh-guh-ree]
» *TRAVEL TIP: will sell pharmaceutical goods, cosmetics, etc. but not general goods; to get a prescription filled go to an 'Apotheke'* [apo-tay-kuh]
drunk *(adjective)* betrunken [buh-troonken]
dry trocken
dry clean chemisch reinigen [shaymish ry-niggen]
dry cleaner eine chemische Reinigung [shay-mish-uh ry-niggoong]
due: when is the bus due? wann soll der Bus ankommen? [van zoll dair booss...]
Durchfahrt verboten no through road
Durchgangsverkehr through traffic
during während [vair-rent]
Duschen showers
dust der Staub [shtōwp]

ELECTRIC 39

Dutch holländisch [hol-end-ish]
Dutchman Holländer [hol-ender]
Dutchwoman Holländerin [hol-enderin]
duty-free *(noun)* das Duty-free
each: may we have one each? können wir jeder eins haben? [kurrnen veer yay-der ine-ts hah-ben]
 how much is each one? was kosten sie pro Stück? [vass kosten zee proh shtōōk]
ear das Ohr [or]
 I have an earache ich habe Ohrenschmerzen [ish hah-buh or-ren-shmairtsen]
early früh [frōō]
 we want to leave a day earlier wir möchten einen Tag früher abreisen [veer murrshten ine-en tahg frōō-uh app-ry-zen]
earring der Ohrring [or-ring]
east der Osten
Easter Ostern [oh-stern]
easy leicht [lysht]
eat essen
 something to eat etwas zu essen [etvass tsoo . . .]
egg ein Ei [eye]
eggplant eine Aubergine [–eenuh]
Einbahnstraße one-way street
Einfahrt (to) highway
Eingang entrance
einordnen get in lane
Einstieg vorn/hinten enter at the front/rear
Eintritt frei admission free
either: either ... or ... entweder ... oder [ent-vay-der oh-der]
 I don't like either mir gefällt beides nicht [meer gheh-fellt by-dess nisht]
elastic elastisch
elbow der Ellbogen [el-boh-ghen]
electric elektrisch
 electric blanket eine Heizdecke [hites-deckuh]
 electric outlet die Steckdose [schteck-doh-zuh]

40 ELECTRICIAN

electrician der Elektriker
electricity die Elektrizität [elek-trits-i-tayt]
» *TRAVEL TIP: voltage is 220 AC*
elegant elegant [el-ay-gannt]
elevator der Aufzug [ōwf-tsoog]
else: something else etwas anderes
  [etvass . . .]
  somewhere else irgendwo anders
  [eer-ghent-voh . . .]
  let's go somewhere else gehen wir woanders
  hin! [gay-en veer vo . . .]
  who else? wer sonst? [vair zonnst]
  or else sonst
embarrassed verlegen [fair-lay-ghen]
embarrassing peinlich [pine-lish]
embassy die Botschaft [boht-shafft]
emergency der Notfall [noht-fal]
emergency brake *(in car)* die Handbremse
  [hannt-brem-zuh]
  (in train) die Notbremse [noht–]
empty leer [layr]
enclose: I enclose . . . ich lege . . . bei
end das Ende
  when does it end? bis wann geht es? [biss van
  gayt ess]
engaged *(to be married)* verlobt
  [fair-lohpt]
engagement ring der Verlobungsring
engine die Maschine [mash-ee-nuh]
  (of car, plane) der Motor [moh-tor]
  engine trouble Schwierigkeiten mit dem
  Motor [shvee-rish-kite-en mit daym . . .]
England England [eng-glannt]
English englisch
  the English die Engländer [eng-glender]
  Englishman Engländer
  Englishwoman Engländerin
enjoy: I enjoyed it very much ich habe es sehr
  genossen [ish hah-buh ess zair gheh–]
  enjoy yourself viel Spaß! [feel shpass]
  I enjoy traveling/driving ich reise/fahre
  gern [ish ry-zuh/fah-ruh gairn]

EVER 41

enlargement *(photo)* die Vergrößerung [fair-gru*rr*ss-eroong]
enormous enorm [ay-norm]
enough genug [geh-noog]
   thank you, that's enough danke, das reicht [dankuh dass rysht]
entertainment die Unterhaltung [oonter-h*a*lt-oong]
entrance der Eingang [ine-gang]
entry der Eintritt [ine–]
entry permit *(for East Germany)* der Passierschein [pas-*ee*r-shine]
envelope ein Umschlag [oom-shlahg]
equipment die Ausrüstung [ōwss-rōōst-oong]
   electrical equipment Elektrogeräte [–gheh-r*a*yt-uh]
eraser ein (Radier)gummi [(radeer)goom-ee]
Erdgeschoß first floor
Erfrischungen refreshments
error der Fehler [fayler]
erste Hilfe first aid
Erwachsene adults
escalator die Rolltreppe [–puh]
especially besonders [buh-zonnders]
essential notwendig [noht-ven-dish]
   it is essential that... es ist unbedingt erforderlich, daß ... [ess ist oon-buh-dingt air-ford-uh-lish dass]
Europe Europa [oy-roh-pa]
European europäisch [oy-roh-p*a*y-ish]
   the Europeans die Europäer [oy-roh-p*a*yer]
evacuate evakuieren [ay-vak-oo-*ee*-ren]
even: even the Americans sogar die Amerikaner [zoh-gar dee am-ay-ree-k*a*h-ner]
evening der Abend [ah-bent]
   good evening guten Abend [gooten ...]
   this evening heute abend [hoytuh ...]
evening dress der Abendanzug [–an-tsoog]
   (woman's) das Abendkleid [–klite]
ever: have you ever been to...? sind Sie jemals in ... gewesen? [zinnt zee yay-malts in ... gheh-v*a*y-zen]

42 EVERY

every jeder [yay-duh]
  every day jeden Tag [yay-den tahg]
everyone jeder
  is everyone ready? sind alle fertig? [zinnt al-uh fair-tish]
everything alles [al-ess]
everywhere überall [ōōber-al]
evidence der Beweis [buh-vice]
exact(ly) genau [gheh-nōw]
example das Beispiel [by-shpeel]
  for example zum Beispiel [tsoom ...]
excellent ausgezeichnet [ōwss-gheh-tsysh-net]
except: except me außer mir [ōwss-uh meer]
excess: excess baggage Übergewicht [ōōber-gheh-visht]
  excess fare die Nachlösegebühr [nahk-lurr-zuh-gheh-bōōr]
exchange *(for money)* die Wechselstube [vek-sel-shtooh-buh]
exciting aufregend [ōwf-ray-ghent]
excursion der Ausflug [ōwss-floog]
  excursion ticket verbilligte Fahrkarte [fair-bill-ishtuh fahr-kartuh]
excuse: excuse me entschuldigen Sie! [ent-shool-dig-en zee]
exhaust *(car)* der Auspuff [ōwss-poof]
exhausted erschöpft [air-shupft]
exhibition die Ausstellung [ōwss-shtel-oong]
exhibitor der Aussteller [ōwss-shteller]
exit der Ausgang [ōwss-gang]
expect erwarten [air-varten]
  she's expecting sie ist in anderen Umständen [zee ist in an-duh-ren oom-shtenden]
expenses die Kosten
  it goes on the expense account das geht auf Spesen [dass gayt ōwf shpay-zen]
expensive teuer [toy-er]
expert der Experte [–pair-tuh]
explain erklären [air-klairen]
  would you explain that slowly? könnten Sie das langsam erklären? [kurrnten zee dass ...]
export *(noun)* der Export

exposure meter der Belichtungsmesser [buh-l*i*shtoongs–]
extra zusätzlich [tsoo-zets-lish]
  an extra glass/day ein Glas/Tag extra [ine glahss/tahg ex-trah]
  is that extra? wird das extra berechnet? [veert dass ... buh-re sh-net]
extremely äußerst [oyss–]
eye das Auge [ōw-guh]
eyebrow die Augenbraue [ōw-ghen-brōw-uh]
eyeliner der Lidstrich [leet-shtrish]
eye shadow der Lidschatten [leet-shat-en]
eyewitness der Augenzeuge [ōw-ghen-tsoy-guh]
face das Gesicht [gheh-*zi*sht]
fact die Tatsache [taht-zah*k*-uh]
factory die Fabrik [fab-re ek]
Fahrenheit Fahrenheit

» *TRAVEL TIP: to convert F to C:* $F - 32 \times \dfrac{5}{9} = C$

Fahrenheit	14	23	32	50	59	70	86	98.4
centigrade	−10	−5	0	10	15	21	30	36.9

Fahrkarten *tickets*
faint: she's fainted sie ist ohnmächtig geworden [zee ist ohn-mesh-tish gheh-vorden]
fair *(carnival)* der Jahrmarkt [yah–] *(commercial)* die Messe [mess-uh]
  that's not fair das ist nicht fair
faithfully: yours faithfully hochachtungsvoll
fake *(noun)* eine Fälschung [fell-shoong]
fall[1] fallen [fal-en]
  he's fallen er ist gefallen [air ist gheh–]
fall[2] der Herbst [hairpst]
  in the fall im Herbst
false falsch
family die Familie [fam-*ee*-lee-uh]
fan der Ventilator [–*a*h-tor] *(soccer, etc.)* der Fan [fen]
fan belt der Keilriemen [kile-ree-men]
far weit [vite]
  is it far? ist es weit? [ist ess vite]
  how far is it? wie weit ist es? [vee ...]

44 FARE

fare *(travel)* der Fahrpreis [fahr-price]
  (on plane) der Flugpreis [floog-price]
farm der Bauernhof [bōw-ern-hohf]
farther weiter [vy–]
fashion die Mode [moh-duh]
fast schnell
  don't speak so fast sprechen Sie nicht so schnell! [shpreshen zee nisht zoh . . .]
fat dick
  (noun) das Fett
fatally tödlich [turrt-lish]
father: my father mein Vater [mine fah-ter]
faucet der Hahn
fault der Fehler [fayler]
  it's not my fault das ist nicht meine Schuld [dass ist nisht mine-uh shoolt]
faulty defekt [dayfekt]
favorite *(adjective)* Lieblings– [leep-lings]
  my favorite city meine Lieblingsstadt [mine-uh leep-lings-shtatt]
February Februar [fay-broo-ar]
fed up: I'm fed up mir reicht's [meer ryshts]
feel: I feel cold/hot/sad mir ist kalt/heiß/ich bin irgendwie traurig [meer ist kalt/hice/ish bin eer-ghent-vee trōw-rish]
  I feel like . . . ich habe Lust auf . . . [ish hah-buh loost ōwf]
Feierabend! we're closing
Fernsprecher telephone
ferry die Fähre [fay-ruh]
Feuermelder fire alarm
fever das Fieber [feeber]
few wenige [vay-nig-uh]
  only a few nur ein paar [noor ine pahr]
  a few days ein paar Tage [ine pahr tah-guh]
fiancé: my fiancé mein Verlobter [mine fair-lohp-ter]
fiancée: my fiancée meine Verlobte [mine-uh fair-lohp-tuh]
field das Feld [fellt]
  (grass) die Wiese [vee-zuh]
fifty-fifty fifty-fifty

FIRST 45

figure die Zahl [tsahl]
 (of person) die Figur [fig-oor]
 I'm watching my figure ich muß auf meine Figur achten [ish mooss ōwf mine-uh ... ah*k*-ten]
fill füllen [fōōl-en]
 fill her up volltanken, bitte [foll– bittuh]
 to fill out a form ein Formular ausfüllen [... ōwss-fōōl-en]
fillet das Filet [feel*ay*]
filling *(tooth)* eine Plombe [plom-buh]
film der Film
 do you have this type of film? haben Sie solche Filme? [hah-ben zee zolshuh ...]
filter: filter or non-filter? mit oder ohne Filter? [... oh-der oh-nuh ...]
find finden [fin-den]
 if you find it ... wenn Sie es finden ... [ven zee ess ...]
 I've found a ... ich habe ein ... gefunden [ish hah-buh ine ... gheh-fōōnden]
fine: fine weather schönes Wetter [shurrn-ess vetter]
 a 50 marks fine eine Geldbuße von fünfzig Mark [ine-uh ghellt-boo-zuh fon fōōnf-tsish ...]
 OK, that's fine das ist gut [dass ist goot]
finger der Finger [fing-uh]
fingernail der Fingernagel [–nah-ghel]
Finland Finnland [fin-lannt]
finish: I haven't finished ich bin noch nicht fertig [ish bin no*k* nisht fair-tish]
fire: fire! Feuer! [foy-er]
 can we light a fire here? können wir hier ein Feuer anzünden? [kurrnen veer heer ine ... an-tsōōnden]
fire department die Feuerwehr [–vair]
 » *TRAVEL TIP: dial 112*
fire extinguisher der Feuerlöscher [–lurrscher]
firm *(noun)* die Firma [feer-mah]
first erste [air-stuh]
 I was first ich war erster [ish var ...]

46 FIRST AID

on the first floor im Erdgeschoß [im airt-gheh-shoss]
first aid Erste Hilfe [air-stuh hill-fuh]
  first aid kit der Verbandskasten [fair-ba*nn*ts–]
first class erster Klasse [air-stuh klass-uh]
first name der Vorname [for-nah-muh]
fish der Fisch
fishing das Angeln [ang-eln]
  fishing rod/tackle die Angelrute/das Angelzeug [ang-el-rootuh/–tsoyg]
fix: can you fix it? *(repair)* können Sie das reparieren? [kurrnen zee dass rep-a-r*ee*-ren] *(arrange)* können Sie das arrangieren? [... ar-ron-dj*ee*-ren]
flag die Fahne [fah-nuh]
  (national, ship's) die Flagge [flag-uh]
flash *(phot)* das Blitzlicht [–lisht]
flashlight eine Taschenlampe [tashen-lamp-uh]
flat flach [flah*k*]
  this drink is flat das schmeckt abgestanden [dass ... app-gheh-shtanden]
  I've got a flat (tire) ich habe einen Platten [ish hah-buh ine-en ...]
flavor der Geschmack [gheh-shm*a*ck]
flea der Floh
flight der Flug [floog]
flirt *(verb)* flirten
float schwimmen [shvimmen]
floor der Boden [boh-den]
  on the third floor im zweiten Stock [... tsvy-ten shtock]
» *TRAVEL TIP: Europeans call the second floor the first floor, the third floor the second floor, etc.*
flower die Blume [bloo-muh]
flu die Grippe [grip-uh]
fly *(insect)* die Fliege [flee-guh]
  (on pants) der Reißverschluß [rice-fair-shl*oo*ss]
foggy neblig [nay-blish]
follow folgen [foll-ghen]
  follow me folgen Sie mir [... zee meer]

FREIGHT 47

food das Essen
  (groceries) die Lebensmittel [lay-benz–]
  see pages 72–73
food poisoning Lebensmittelvergiftung
  [lay-benz-mittel-fair-ghif-toong]
fool der Narr
foot der Fuß [fooss]
» *TRAVEL TIP: 1 foot = 30.1 cm = 0.3 meters*
for für [főr]
forbidden verboten [fair-boh-ten]
foreign ausländisch [ōwss-lend-ish]
foreign exchange Devisen [day-vee-zen]
foreigner ein Ausländer [ōwss-lender]
forest der Wald [valt]
forget vergessen [fair-ghessen]
  I forget, I've forgotten ich habe es vergessen
  [ish hah-buh ess . . .]
  don't forget vergessen Sie nicht [. . . zee
  nisht]
  I'll never forget you ich werde dich nie
  vergessen [. . . vair-duh dish nee . . .]
fork die Gabel [gah-bel]
form *(document)* das Formular [form-oo-lar]
formal formell
  (person, manner) förmlich [furrm-lish]
forward *(adverb)* vorwärts [for-vairts]
  forwarding address die Nachsendeadresse
  [nahk-zenduh-ad-ressuh]
  could you forward my mail? könnten Sie
  mir die Post nachsenden? [kurrnten zee meer
  dee posst nahk-zenden]
foundation cream die Grundierungscreme
  [groon-deer-roongs-kray-muh]
fracture der Bruch [brook]
fragile zerbrechlich [tsair-bresh-lish]
France Frankreich [–rysh]
fraud der Betrug [buh-troog]
free frei [fry]
  admission free Eintritt frei [ine–]
frei free
Freibad outdoor pool
freight die Fracht [frahkt]

48 FREMDENZIMMER

Fremdenzimmer rooms
French französisch [frants-*u*rr-zish]
  (person) Franzose [frants-*oh*-zuh]
  (woman) Französin [frants-*u*rrs-zin]
French fries die Pommes frites [pom freet]
fresh *(fruit, etc.)* frisch [frish]
  (impudent) frech [fresh]
  don't get fresh! was erlauben Sie sich! [vass air-lōw-ben zee zish]
freshen up: I want to freshen up ich möchte mich frischmachen [ish murrshtuh mish frish-mah*k*-en]
friction tape das Isolierband [eez-oh-*lee*er-bannt]
Friday Freitag [fry-tahg]
friend ein Freund [froynt]
friendly freundlich [froynt-lish]
from von [fon]
  from America aus Amerika [ōwss am-*ay*-ree-kah]
  where is it from? wo kommt es her? [voh . . . ess hair]
front *(noun)* die Vorderseite [for-der-zy-tuh]
  in front of you vor Ihnen [for ee-nen]
  in the front vorn [forn]
frost der Frost
frostbite die Frostbeule [–boy-luh]
frozen *(food)* tiefgekühlt [teef-gheh-kōōlt]
  (person) eiskalt [ice–]
fruit das Obst [ohpst]
fruit salad der Obstsalat [ohpst-zal-*a*ht]
fry braten [brah-ten]
  nothing fried nichts Gebratenes [nix gheh-br*a*h-ten-ess]
  fried egg ein Spiegelei [shpee-ghel-eye]
frying pan die Bratpfanne [braht-pfann-uh]
full voll [foll]
fun: it's fun das macht Spaß [dass mah*k*t shpass]
Fundbüro lost and found
funny *(strange, comical)* komisch [koh–]
furniture die Möbel [murr-bel]
further weiter [vy–]

GERMANY

fuse die Sicherung [zisher-oong]
future die Zukunft [tsoo-koonft]
gale der Sturm [shtoorm]
gallon die Gallone [gal-oh-nuh]
  » *TRAVEL TIP: 1 gallon = 3.8 liters*
gallstone ein Gallenstein [gal-en-shtine]
gamble spielen [shpee-len]
  (on horses) wetten [vet-en]
garage *(repair)* die Werkstatt [vairk-shtatt]
  (parking) die Garage [ga-rah-djuh]
garden der Garten
garlic der Knoblauch [kuh-nohp-lōwk]
gas *(gasoline)* das Benzin [ben-tseen]
  gas cylinder der Gaszylinder [–tsoo-linnder]
  gas pedal das Gas
  gas station eine Tankstelle [–shtel-uh]
gasket die Dichtung [dish-toong]
gay *(homosexual)* schwul [shvool]
gear der Gang
  (equipment) die Ausrüstung
  [ōwss-rōos-toong]
  I can't get it into gear ich kann den Gang
  nicht einlegen [ish kan dayn ... nisht
  ine-lay-ghen]
  gear shift der Schaltknüppel [–kuh-nōo-pel]
  (column-mounted) der Schalthebel [–hay-bel]
Gebühren charges
Gefahr danger
Gegenverkehr oncoming traffic
general delivery postlagernd
  [posst-lah-ghernt]
gentleman: the gentleman who ... der Herr,
  der ... [dair hair dair]
geöffnet open
Gepäckaufbewahrung baggage checkroom
German deutsch [doytsh]
  (person) Deutscher
  (woman) Deutsche [doytsh-uh]
  I don't speak German ich spreche kein
  Deutsch [ish shpresh-uh kine doytsh]
  the Germans die Deutschen
Germany Deutschland [doytsh-lannt]

50 GESCHLOSSEN

geschlossen *closed*
Geschwindigkeitsbegrenzung *speed limit*
gesture eine Geste [ghay-stuh]
get: will you get me a ...? holen Sie mir bitte ein ...? [hoh-len zee meer bittuh ine]
  how do I get to? wie komme ich zu ...? [vee komm-uh ish tsoo]
  when can I get it back? wann bekomme ich es zurück? [van buh-komm-uh ish ess tsoo-rōōk]
  where do I get off? wo muß ich aussteigen? [voh mooss ish ōwss-shty-ghen]
  when do we get back? wann sind wir zurück? [van zinnt veer tsoo-rōōk]
  where do I get a bus for ...? wo fährt der Bus nach ...? [voh fairt dair booss nahk ... app]
  will you come and get me? werden Sie mich abholen? [vairden zee mish app-hoh-len]
  have you got ...? haben Sie ...? [hah-ben zee]
gift ein Geschenk [geh-shenk]
gin ein Gin
  gin and tonic ein Gin Tonic
girl ein Mädchen [mayd-shen]
  my girlfriend meine Freundin [mine-uh froyn-din]
give geben [gay-ben]
  I gave it to him ich habe es ihm gegeben [ish hah-buh ess eem gheh-gay-ben]
glad froh
glass das Glas
  a glass of water ein Glas Wasser [vasser]
glasses *(eye)* die Brille [brill-uh]
Glatteis *icy conditions*
Gleis *track*
gloves die Handschuhe [hannt-shoo-uh]
glue der Klebstoff [klayp-shtoff]
GmbH *Gesellschaft mit beschränkter Haftung Inc.*
go gehen [gay-en]; *(by vehicle)* fahren
  where are you going? wo gehen Sie hin?
  my car won't go mein Auto fährt nicht [mine ōw-toh fairt nisht]

GREECE 51

when does the bus go? wann fährt der Bus? [van fairt dair booss]
YOU MAY THEN HEAR...
 alle zehn Minuten *every ten minutes*
 jede Stunde *every hour*
 he's/it's gone er/es ist weg [air/ess ist vek]
goal *(soccer, etc.)* das Tor
goat die Ziege [tsee-guh]
god Gott
goggles *(ski)* die Schneebrille [shnay-brill-uh]
gold das Gold [gollt]
golf Golf
good gut [goot]
goodbye auf Wiedersehen [ōwf vee-duh-zayn]
gooseberries Stachelbeeren [shtak-el-bay-ren]
gram ein Gramm
» *TRAVEL TIP: 100 gram = approx 3½ oz*
grand großartig [grohss-artish]
 my grandfather mein Großvater [–fah–]
 my grandmother meine Großmutter [–moot–]
 my grandson mein Enkel
 my granddaughter meine Enkelin [eng-kel-in]
grapefruit die Grapefruit
 grapefruit juice ein Grapefruitsaft [–zafft]
grapes Trauben [trōw-ben]
grass das Gras
grateful dankbar
 I'm very grateful to you ich bin Ihnen sehr dankbar [ish bin ee-nen zair ...]
gratitude die Dankbarkeit [–kite]
gravy die Soße [zoh-suh]
gray grau [grōw]
grease das Fett
 (car, etc.) die Wagenschmiere [vah-ghen-shmee-ruh]
greasy fettig [–ish]
great groß
 (very good) großartig [–artish]
 great! klasse! [klass-uh]
Greece Griechenland [greeken-lannt]

52 GREEDY

greedy gierig [ghee-rish]
green grün [grōōn]
grocery store der Kaufmann [kōwf--]
ground der Boden [boh-den]
  on the ground auf dem Boden [ōwf daym ...]
ground beef der Hackfleisch [--flysh]
group die Gruppe [grōōp-uh]
  our group leader unser Gruppenleiter [ōōn-zer grōōpen-ly-ter]
  I'm with the American group ich gehöre zur amerikanischen Gruppe [ish geh-hurr-uh tsoor am-ay-ree-kah-nish-en ...]
guarantee die Garantie
  is there a guarantee? bekommen wir eine Garantie? [buh-kommen veer ine-uh ...]
guest der Gast
guide der Führer [fōōruh]
guilty schuldig [shōōl-dish]
guitar die Gitarre [ghee-ta-ruh]
gum (around teeth) der Gaumen [gōw-men]
  see **chewing gum**
gun das Gewehr [gheh-vair]
  (pistol) die Pistole [--oh-luh]
gynecologist der Gynäkologe [gōō-nay-koh-loh-guh]
hair das Haar
  hairbrush die Haarbürste [--bōōr-stuh]
  where can I get a haircut? wo kann ich mir die Haare schneiden lassen? [voh kan ish meer dee hah-ruh shnyden lassen]
  is there a hairdresser here? gibt es hier einen Friseur? [gheept ess heer ine-en free-zurr]
» TRAVEL TIP: *hairdressers close on Mondays*
half halb [halp]
  a half portion eine halbe Portion [hal-buh portsee-ohn]
  half an hour eine halbe Stunde [... shtōōn-duh]
halt stop
ham der Schinken
hamburger ein Hamburger

HAVE 53

hammer ein Hammer
hand die Hand [hannt]
handbag die Handtasche [hannt-tash-uh]
hand baggage das Handgepäck [hannt-gheh-peck]
handkerchief das Taschentuch [tash-en-took]
handle der Griff
 will you handle it? kümmern Sie sich bitte darum? [kööm-ern zee zish bittuh da-room]
handmade handgearbeitet [hannt-gheh-ar-by-tet]
handsome gutaussehend [goot-ōwss-zay-ent]
hanger der Kleiderbügel [kly-der-bōō-gel]
hangover der Kater [kahter]
 my head is splitting mir platzt fast der Kopf [meer ... fasst dair ...]
happen geschehen [gheh-shay-en]
 I don't know how it happened ich weiß nicht, wie es geschehen ist [ish vice nisht vee ess ...]
 what's happening/happened? was ist los? [vass ist lohss]
happy glücklich [glōōk-lish]
harbor der Hafen [hah-fen]
hard hart
 (difficult) schwierig [shvee-rish]
hard-boiled egg ein hartgekochtes Ei [–gheh-ko*k*-tes eye]
hardware store die (Eisen- und) Haushaltswarenhandlung [(eye-zen oont) hōwss-halts-vah-ren-hannt-loong]
harm der Schaden [shah-den]
hat der Hut [hoot]
 (knitted) die Mütze [mōōt-suh]
hate: I hate ... ich hasse ... [ish hass-uh]
have haben [hah-ben]
 I don't have time ich habe keine Zeit [ish hah-buh kine-uh tsite]
 do you have any cigars/a map? haben Sie Zigarren/eine Karte? [hah-ben zee ...]

54 HAY FEVER

may I have some water/some more? kann ich etwas Wasser/noch ein bißchen haben? [kan ish etvass vasser/no*k* ine biss-shen hah-ben]
I have to leave tomorrow ich muß morgen abreisen [ish mooss mor-ghen app-ry-zen]
have a nice day/evening schönen Tag/Abend noch [shurrnen tahg/ah-bent no*k*]
hay fever der Heuschnupfen [hoy-shnoop-fen]
Hbf Hauptbahnhof *main station*
he er [air]
  he is er ist
head der Kopf
headache Kopfschmerzen [--schmair-tsen]
headlight der Scheinwerfer [shine-vairfer]
head waiter der Oberkellner [ohber--]
health die Gesundheit [geh-z∞nt-hite]
  to your health! auf Ihr Wohl! [ōwf eer vohl]
healthy gesund [geh-z∞nt]
hear: I can't hear ich höre nichts [ish hurr-uh nix]
hearing aid das Hörgerät [hurr-gheh-rayt]
heart das Herz [hairts]
heart attack ein Herzinfarkt [hairts--]
heat die Hitze [hit-suh]
heating die Heizung [hites-∞ng]
heat stroke ein Hitzschlag [hits-shlahg]
heavy schwer [shvair]
heel der Absatz [app-zats]
  could you put new heels on these? könnten Sie neue Absätze darauf machen? [kurrnten zee noy-uh app-zets-uh dah-rōwf mah*k*en]
height die Höhe [hurr-uh]
  (person's) die Größe [grurr-suh]
heiß *hot*
hello hallo
helmet *(motorcycle)* der Sturzhelm [shtoorts-helm]
help helfen
  can you help me? würden Sie mir helfen? [vōōrden zee meer . . .]
  help! Hilfe! [hill-fuh]

HONEYMOON 55

her sie [zee]
  will you give it to her? würden Sie es ihr geben? [vūrden zee ess eer gay-ben]
  it's her bag, it's hers es ist ihre Tasche, es ist ihre [ess ist ee-ruh tash-uh]
here hier [heer]
  come here komm her! [. . . hair]
Herren men's rest room
high hoch [hoh*k*]
high beam das Fernlicht [fairn-lisht]
highway die Autobahn [ōwtoh-bahn]
hill der Berg [bairk]
  up/down the hill den Berg hinauf/hinunter [dayn . . . hin-ōwf/hin-∞nter]
him ihn [een]
  will you give it to him? würden Sie es ihm geben? [vūrden zee ess eem gay-ben]
  it's him er ist es [air ist ess]
his sein [zine]
  it's his drink, it's his es ist sein Drink, es ist seiner [ess ist zine-uh]
hit: he hit me er hat mich geschlagen [air hat mish gheh-shl*a*h-ghen]
hitchhike trampen [trempen]
hitchhiker der Anhalter
Hochgarage multi-level parking garage
Höchstgeschwindigkeit maximum speed
hold halten
hole das Loch [lo*k*]
holiday der Feiertag [fy-er-tahg]
Holland Holland [holl-annt]
home das Zuhause [tsoo-hōw-zuh]
  I want to go home ich möchte nach Hause [ish murrshtuh nah*k* hōw-zuh]
  at home zu Hause
  I'm homesick ich habe Heimweh [ish hah-buh hime-vay]
honest ehrlich [air-lish]
  honestly? ehrlich?
honey der Honig [hoh-nish]
honeymoon die Hochzeitsreise [hoc*k*-tsites-ry-zuh]

56 HOOD

hood *(of car)* die Motorhaube [moh-tor-hōwbuh]
hope die Hoffnung [hoff-noong]
  I hope that... ich hoffe, daß... [ish hoff-uh dass]
  I hope so/not hoffentlich/hoffentlich nicht! [hoff-ent-lish]
horizon der Horizont [horee-tsonnt]
horn *(car)* die Hupe [hoo-puh]
horrible schrecklich [–lish]
hors d'oeuvre das Hors d'oeuvre
horse das Pferd [pfairt]
hospital das Krankenhaus [–hōwss]
host der Gastgeber [–gay-ber]
hostess die Gastgeberin [–gay-ber-in]
hot heiß [hice]
  (spiced) scharf
hot dog ein Hot dog
hotel das Hotel
hotplate die Wärmplatte [vairm-plat-uh]
hot-water bottle die Wärmflasche [vairm-flash-uh]
hour eine Stunde [shtoon-duh]
house das Haus [hōwss]
housewife eine Hausfrau [hōwss-frōw]
how wie [vee]
  how many wieviele [vee-feel-uh]
  how much wieviel [vee-feel]
  how often wie oft
  how long wie lange [... lang-uh]
  how long have you been here? seit wann sind Sie da? [zite van zinnt zee dah]
  how are you? wie geht's? [vee gayts]
humid feucht [foysht]
humor der Humor [hoo-mor]
hungry hungrig [hoon-grish]
  I'm hungry/not hungry ich habe Hunger/ich habe keinen Hunger [ish hah-buh hoong-er/... kine-en ...]
hupen *sound your horn*
hurry: I'm in a hurry ich habe es eilig [ish hah-buh ess eye-lish]

IMPROVE 57

please hurry! bitte beeilen Sie sich! [bittuh buh-*eye*-len zee zish]
hurt: it hurts es tut weh [ess toot vay]
  my leg hurts mein Bein tut mir weh [mine bine toot meer vay]
  YOU MAY HEAR ...
  ist es ein stechender Schmerz? [ist ess ine shtesh-ender shmairts] *is it a sharp pain?*
husband: my husband mein Mann [mine ...]
I ich [ish]
  I am ich bin
ice das Eis [ice]
  with lots of ice mit viel Eis [mit feel ...]
ice ax der Eispickel [ice–]
ice cream ein Eis [ice]
iced coffee ein Eiskaffee [ice-kaff-ay]
iced tea ein Eistee [ice-tay]
ice water Eiswasser [ice-vasser]
identity papers die Ausweispapiere [ōwss-vice-pap-*ee*-ruh]
idiot der Idiot [id-ee-oht]
if wenn [ven]
ignition die Zündung [tsoon-doong]
ill krank
  I feel ill ich fühle mich nicht wohl [ish fōō-luh mish nisht vohl]
illegal illegal [ill-ay-g*a*hl]
illegible unleserlich [oon-*l*ay-zair-lish]
illness die Krankheit [–hite]
Imbiß(stube) snack bar
immediately sofort [zohfort]
import der Import
important wichtig [vish-tish]
  it's very important es ist sehr wichtig [ess ist zair ...]
import duty der Einfuhrzoll [ine-foor-tsoll]
impossible unmöglich [oon-m*u*rr-glish]
impressive beeindruckend [buh-*ine*-drook-ent]
improve verbessern [fairb*e*ssern]
  I want to improve my German ich möchte besser Deutsch lernen [ish murrshtuh besser doytsh lair-nen]

58 IN

in in
inch der Zoll [tsoll]
» *TRAVEL TIP: 1 inch = 2.54 cm*
include einschließen [ine-shlee-sen]
  does that include breakfast? ist Frühstück
  inbegriffen? [ist frōō-shtōōk in-buh–]
inclusive inklusive [in-kloo-zee-vuh]
incompetent unfähig [ōōn-fay-ish]
inconsiderate unaufmerksam
  [ōōn-ōwf-mairk-zahm]
incredible unglaublich [ōōn-glōwp-lish]
indecent unanständig [ōōn-an-shtendish]
independent unabhängig [ōōn-app-heng-ish]
indigestion die Magenverstimmung
  [mah-ghen-fair-shtim-ōōng]
indoors drinnen
industry die Industrie [in-dōos-tree]
infection die Infektion [in-fekts-ee-ohn]
infectious ansteckend [an-shteck-ent]
inflation die Inflation [in-flats-ee-ohn]
informal zwanglos [tsvang-lohs]
  (dress) leger [lay-jair]
  (agreement) informell
information Informationen
  [in-for-mats-ee-oh-nen]
  **do you have any information in English
  on . . . ?** haben Sie Informationsmaterial auf
  Englisch über . . . ? [. . .–mah-tay-ree-ahl ōwf
  eng-glish ōōber]
  is there an information office? gibt es da
  eine Informationsbüro? [gheept ess dah ine-uh
  –bōōroh]
inhabitant der Einwohner [ine-voh-ner]
injection die Spritze [shprits-uh]
injured verletzt [fair-letst]
  he's been injured er ist verletzt
injury die Verletzung [fair-lets-ōōng]
innocent unschuldig [ōōn-shool-dish]
insect ein Insekt [inzekt]
inside innen
insist: I insist (on it) ich bestehe darauf [ish
  buh-shtay-uh dah-rōwf]

ITALY 59

insomnia die Schlaflosigkeit
 [shlahf-lohs-ish-kite]
instant coffee der Pulverkaffee
 [pool-ver-kaff-ay]
instead statt dessen [shtatt . . .]
 instead of anstelle von [an-shtel-uh fon]
insulation die Isolierung [eez-oh-leeroong]
insult die Beleidigung [buh-lide-ee-goong]
insurance die Versicherung [fair-zish-eroong]
intelligent intelligent [–ghent]
interesting interessant [–ant]
international international
 [inter-nats-ee-oh-nahl]
**interpret: would you interpret for
 us?** würden Sie für uns dolmetschen? [voorden
 zee foor oonts doll-met-shen]
intersection die Kreuzung [kroy-tsoong]
into in
introduce: may I introduce . . . ? darf
 ich . . . vorstellen? [. . . for-shtellen]
invalid (noun) der Kranke [–kuh]
 (disabled) der Invalide [in-val-eeduh]
invitation die Einladung [ine-lah-doong]
 thank you for the invitation danke für die
 Einladung [dankuh foor dee . . .]
invite: may I invite you out tonight? kann ich
 Sie für heute abend einladen? [kan ish zee foor
 hoytuh ah-bent ine-la-den]
invoice die Rechnung [resh-noong]
Ireland Irland [eer-lannt]
iron (verb) bügeln [boo-geln]
 (noun) das Bügeleisen [–eye-zen]
 will you iron these for me? würden Sie diese
 für mich bügeln? [voorden zee deez-uh foor
 mish . . .]
is ist [ist]
island die Insel [in-zel]
it es [ess]
Italian italienisch [it-al-ee-ay-nish]
 (person) Italiener
 (woman) Italienerin
Italy Italien [i-tahl-ee-un]

60 ITCH

itch: it itches es juckt [. . . yoockt]
itemize: would you itemize it for me? würden Sie dies für mich aufschlüsseln? [vōorden zee deess fōor mish ōwf-shlōos-eln]
jack der Wagenheber [vah-ghen-hay-ber]
jacket die Jacke [yack-uh]
 (of man's suit) das Jackett
jam die Marmelade [mar-meh-lah-duh]
 traffic jam der (Verkehrs)stau [fair-kayrs-shtōw]
January Januar [yan-oo-ar]
jaw der Kiefer [kee-fer]
jealous eifersüchtig [eye-fair-zōosh-tish]
jeans die Jeans
jellyfish die Qualle [kvalluh]
jetty der Pier
jewelry der Schmuck [shmoock]
job die Arbeit [ar-bite]
joke *(noun)* der Witz [vits]
 you must be joking das soll wohl ein Witz sein [dass zol vohl ine vits zine]
July Juli [yoo-lee]
jumper cables Starthilfekabel [shtart-hill-fuh-kah-bel]
junction die Kreuzung [kroy-tsoong]
June Juni [yoo-nee]
junk der Ramsch [ramsh]
just: just two nur zwei [noor tsvy]
 just a little nur ein wenig [noor ine vayn-ish]
 that's just right das ist gerade richtig [dass ist geh-rah-duh rish-tish]
 he was here just now er war gerade hier [air var geh-rah-duh heer]
kalt cold
Kasse cash register
keep: may I keep it? kann ich es behalten? [. . . buh-halten]
 you keep it Sie können es behalten [zee kurrnen . . .]
 keep the change der Rest ist für Sie [dair rest ist fōor zee]

you didn't keep your promise Sie haben Ihr
Versprechen nicht gehalten [zee hah-ben eer
fair-shpresher nisht gheh-hɑlten]
 it keeps on breaking es geht dauernd kaputt
[ess gayt dōw-ernt ...]
kein Durchgang für Fußgänger *no pedestrians*
kein Trinkwasser *not for drinking*
kein Zutritt (für Unbefugte) *no admittance (for unauthorized persons)*
ketchup das Ketchup
key der Schlüssel [shlōōs-el]
kidney die Niere [nee-ruh]
kill töten [turr-ten]
kilo ein Kilo

» *TRAVEL TIP: conversion:* $\frac{kilos}{5} \times 11 = pounds$

| kilos | 1 | 1½ | 5 | 6 | 7 | 8 | 9 |
| pounds | 2.2 | 3.3 | 11 | 13.2 | 15.4 | 17.6 | 19.8 |

kilometer ein Kilometer [–may-ter]

» *TRAVEL TIP: conversion:* $\frac{kilometers}{8} \times 5 = miles$

| kilometers | 1 | 5 | 10 | 20 | 50 | 100 |
| miles | 0.62 | 3.11 | 6.2 | 12.4 | 31 | 62 |

kind: that's very kind of you das ist sehr
freundlich von Ihnen [... zair froynt-lish fon
ee-nen]
kiss der Kuß [kœss]
kitchen die Küche [kōō-shuh]
knee das Knie [kuh-n*ee*]
knife ein Messer
knock klopfen
 the engine is knocking der Motor klopft
know wissen [vissen]
 (be acquainted with) kennen
 I don't know ich weiß nicht
 [ish vice nisht]
 I know him ich kenne ihn [... ken-uh een]
Krankenhaus *hospital*
Kreuzung *intersection*
kurvenreiche Strecke *winding road*
label das Etikett
lacquer der Lack

62 LADIES' ROOM

ladies' room die Damentoilette [dah-men-twa-lettuh]
lady eine Dame [dah-muh]
lake der See [zay]
lamb *(meat)* das Lamm
lamp die Lampe [lamp-uh]
lamppost der Laternenpfahl [lah-*tair*n-en-pfahl]
lampshade der Lampenschirm [–sheerm]
land *(noun)* das Land [lannt]
lane *(car)* die Spur [shpoor]
langsam fahren drive slowly
language die Sprache [shprah-*k*uh]
large groß [grohss]
laryngitis die Kehlkopfentzündung [kayl-kopf-ent-tsoon-doong]
last letzter [lets-ter]
 last year/week letztes Jahr/letzte Woche
 last night gestern abend; *(late)* gestern nacht [ghestern ah-bent/nah*k*t]
 last name der Zuname [tsoo-nah-muh]
 at last! endlich! [ent-lish]
late: sorry I'm late entschuldigen Sie, daß ich zu spät komme [ent-sh*oo*l-dig-en zee dass ish tsoo shpayt kommuh]
 it's a bit late es ist ein bißchen spät [... bis-shen ...]
 please hurry, I'm late bitte beeilen Sie sich, ich bin spät dran [bittuh buh-*eye*-len zee zish ish bin shpayt dran]
 at the latest spätestens [shpayt-es-tenz]
 later später [shpayter]
 I'll come back later ich komme später zurück
 see you later! bis später!
laugh *(verb)* lachen [lah-*k*en]
Laundromat die Münzwäscherei [m*oo*nts-vesher-eye]
» *TRAVEL TIP: not very many of these in Germany; try a 'Sofortreinigung' (dry cleaner)*
laundry eine Wäscherei [vesher-ry]
law das Gesetz [geh-*ze*ts]
Lawinengefahr danger of avalanches

lawyer der Rechtsanwalt [reshts-anvalt]
laxative ein Abführmittel [app-foor-mittel]
lazy faul [fowl]
leaf das Blatt
leak eine undichte Stelle [oon-dish-tuh shtel-uh]
   it leaks es ist nicht dicht
learn: I want to learn ich möchte ... lernen [ish murrshtuh ... lair-nen]
lease *(verb)* mieten [meeten]
   (land, business premises) pachten [pak-ten]
least: not in the least nicht im geringsten [nisht im gheringsten]
   at least mindestens [minn-dess-tenz]
leather das Leder [lay-der]
leave: we're leaving tomorrow wir fahren morgen ab [veer fah-ren ... app]
   when does the bus leave? wann fährt der Bus? [van fairt dair booss]
   YOU MAY THEN HEAR ...
   alle zehn Minuten *every ten minutes*
   jede Stunde *every hour*
   I left two shirts in my room ich habe zwei Hemden in meinem Zimmer liegenlassen [ish hah-buh tsvy ... lee-ghen-lassen]
   may I leave this here? kann ich das hierlassen? [... heerlassen]
Lebensgefahr danger
left linke
   on the left links
   to be left-handed Linkshänder sein [links-hender zine]
leg das Bein [bine]
legal legal [lay-gahl]
legal aid die Rechtshilfe [reshts-hil-fuh]
lemon die Zitrone [tsi-troh-nuh]
lemonade eine Limonade [lee-moh-na-duh]
lend: will you lend me your ...? leihen Sie mir Ihr ...? [lye-en zee meer eer ...]
lengthen verlängern [fair-lengern]
   (clothes) länger machen [lenger mah-ken]
lens *(of glasses)* das Glas [glahss]
   (camera) das Objektiv [opp-yek-teef]

64 LENT

Lent die Fastenzeit [fass-ten-tsite]
less weniger [vay-nee-gher]
let: let me help darf ich Ihnen helfen?
 [... ee-nen ...]
 let me go! lassen Sie mich los! [... lohs]
 will you let me off here würden Sie mich hier
 aussteigen lassen [vōorden zee mish heer
 ōwss-shty-ghen ...]
 let's go gehen wir! [gay-en veer]
letter der Brief [breef]
 are there any letters for me? habe ich Post?
 [hah-buh ish posst]
liable *(responsible)* haftbar
library die Bibliothek [biblee-oh-tayk]
license die Genehmigung [gheh-nay-mee-goong]
license plate das Nummernschild
 [noomern-shillt]
lid der Deckel
lie *(noun)* eine Lüge [lōō-guh]
 can he lie down for a while? kann er sich ein
 bißchen hinlegen? [kan air zish ine bis-shen
 hin-lay-ghen]
life das Leben [lay-ben]
life belt der Rettungsgürtel [ret-oongs-gōortel]
lifeboat das Rettungsboot [–boht]
lifeguard der Bademeister [bah-duh-my-ster]
 (on beach) der Rettungsschwimmer
 [–shvimmer]
life insurance die Lebensversicherung
 [lay-benz-fair-zish-er-oong]
life jacket eine Schwimmweste
 [schvim-vest-uh]
light das Licht [lisht]
 (not heavy) leicht [lysht]
 the lights aren't working das Licht geht
 nicht [... gayt nisht]
 (car) die Scheinwerfer funktionieren nicht
 [shine-vairfer foonk-tsee-ohn-ee-ren ...]
 do you have a light? haben Sie Feuer?
 [hah-ben zee foy-er]
 when it gets light wenn es hell wird
 [ven ... veert]

light bulb die Glühbirne [glōō-beer-nuh]
light meter der Belichtungsmesser [buh-lish-toongs-messer]
like: would you like ...? möchten Sie ...? [murrshten zee]
  I'd like a .../I'd like to ... ich hätte gerne ein .../ich würde gerne ... [ish hett-uh gairn-uh ine/vōōrduh ...]
  I like it/you das gefällt mir/ich mag Sie gern [dass gheh-felt meer/ish mahg zee gairn]
  I don't like it das gefällt mir nicht [gheh-felt meer nisht]
  like this one wie dieser [vee dee-zer]
  what's it like? wie ist es? [vee ...]
  do it like this machen Sie es so [mah-ken zee ess zoh]
lime die Limone [lee-moh-nuh]
line die Linie [lee-nee-uh]
  (of people) eine Schlange [shlang-uh]
lip die Lippe [lip-uh]
lipstick der Lippenstift [-shtift]
liqueur ein Likör [lik-urr]
list *(noun)* die Liste [list-uh]
listen zuhören [tsoo-hurr-ren]
  listen! hören Sie zu! [hurr-ren zee tsoo]
liter der Liter [lee-ter]
» *TRAVEL TIP: 1 liter = 1.06 quarts = 0.26 gal*
little klein [kline]
  a little ice/a little more ein wenig Eis/noch ein wenig [ine vay-nish ice/nok ...]
  just a little nur ein wenig, nur ein bißchen [noor ... bis-shen]
live leben [lay-ben]
  I live in ... ich wohne in ... [ish voh-nuh ...]
  where do you live? wo wohnen Sie? [voh voh-nen zee]
liver die Leber [lay-ber]
Lkw = Lastkraftwagen *truck*
loaf ein Brot [broht]
lobby das Foyer [fwy-yay]
lobster ein Hummer [hoommer]

66 LOCAL

local: could we try a local wine? können wir einen Wein aus der Gegend probieren? [kurrnen veer ine-en vine ōwss dair gay-ghent proh-bee-ren]
  a local restaurant ein Restaurant im Ort [... res-tor-rong ...]
  is it made locally? wird es hier hergestellt? [veert ess heer hair-gheh-shtelt]
lock: the lock's broken das Schloß ist kaputt [... shloss ...]
  I've locked myself out ich habe mich ausgeschlossen [ish hah-buh mish ōwss-gheh-shlossen]
lonely einsam [ine-zahm]
long lang
  we'd like to stay longer wir würden gerne etwas länger bleiben [veer vōōrden gairn-uh etvass leng-er bly-ben]
  that was long ago das ist lange her [... lang-uh hair]
look: you look tired Sie sehen müde aus [zee zay-en mōō-duh ōwss]
  I'm looking forward to ... ich freue mich auf ... [ish froy-uh mish ōwf]
  I'm looking for ... ich suche ... [ish zook-uh]
  I'm just looking ich möchte mich nur umschauen [ish murrshtuh mish noor oom-shōw-en]
  look at that schauen Sie sich das an! [shōw-en zee zish dass an]
  look out! Vorsicht! [for-zisht]
loose lose [loh-zuh]
lose verlieren [fair-lee-ren]
  I've lost my ... ich habe mein ... verloren [ish hah-buh mine ... fair-lor-ren]
  excuse me, I'm lost entschuldigen Sie, ich habe mich verlaufen [ent-shool-dig-en zee ish hah-buh mish fair-lōwf-en]
  (driving) ich habe mich verfahren [... fair-fah-ren]
lost and found das Fundbüro [foont-bōō-roh]

MAGNIFICENT 67

lot: a lot/not a lot viel/nicht viel [feel]
   a lot of French fries/wine eine Menge Pommes Frites/Wein [ine-uh meng-uh pom freet/vine]
   lots of jede Menge [yay-duh ...]
   a lot more expensive viel teurer [feel toy-rer]
lotion die Lotion [lohts-ee-ohn]
loud laut [lowt]
   louder lauter [lowter]
love: I love you ich liebe dich [ish lee-buh dish]
   he's in love er ist verliebt [air ist fair-leept]
   I love this wine ich mag diesen Wein sehr gern [ish mahg dee-zen vine zair gairn]
   do you love me? liebst du mich? [leepst doo mish]
lovely schön [shurrn]
low niedrig [nee-drish]
low beam Abblendlicht [app-blent-lisht]
luck das Glück [glōock]
   good luck! viel Glück! [feel glōock]
lucky Glücks- [glōocks-]
   you're lucky Sie haben Glück [zee hah-ben glōock]
   that was lucky Glück gehabt [... geh-hahpt]
lump die Beule [boy-luh]
   (inside) die Geschwulst [geh-shvoolst]
lunch das Mittagessen [mittahg-essen]
   may I have a box lunch? könnte ich ein Lunchpaket haben? [kurrntuh ish ine lunch-pa-kayt hah-ben]
lung die Lunge [loong-uh]
Luxembourg Luxemburg [looxemboorg]
luxurious luxuriös [loox-oo-ree-urrs]
luxury der Luxus [loox-ooss]
machine die Maschine [mash-ee-nuh]
mad verrückt [fair-rōockt]
madam gnädige Frau [guh-nay-dig-uh frow]
made-to-order nach Maß [nahk mahss]
magazine die Zeitschrift [tsite-shrift]
magnificent großartig [grohss-ahr-tish]

68 MAID

maid *(in hotel)* das Zimmermädchen [tsimmer-mayd-shen]
maiden name der Mädchenname [maid-shen-nah-muh]
mail die Post [posst]
　is there any mail for me? habe ich Post? [hah-buh ish . . .]
mailbox der Briefkasten [breef–]
　» TRAVEL TIP: *mailboxes are yellow*
main road die Hauptstraße [hōwpt-shtrahss-uh]
make machen [mah-ken]
　will we make it in time? schaffen wir das rechtzeitig? [shaffen veer dass resht-tsytish]
makeup das Make-up
man der Mann
manager der Geschäftsführer [gheh-shefts-fōōr-er]
　may I see the manager? kann ich den Geschäftsführer sprechen? [. . . shprechen]
manicure die Maniküre [man-ee-kōō-ruh]
manners die Manieren [man-ee-ren]
many viele [feel-uh]
map die Karte [kar-tuh]
　a map of . . . eine Karte von . . . [ine-uh kar-tuh fon]
March März [mairts]
margarine die Margarine [mar-ga-reen-uh]
marina der Jachthafen [yakt-hah-fen]
mark: there's a mark on it es ist beschädigt [. . . buh-shay-disht]
　(stained) da ist ein Fleck darauf [. . . dah-rōwf]
market der Markt
marketplace der Marktplatz
marmalade die Orangenmarmelade [oron-djen-mar-meh-lah-duh]
married verheiratet [fair-hy-raht-et]
marry: will you marry me? willst du mich heiraten? [villst doo mish hy-rahten]
marvelous wunderbar [voonderbar]
mascara die Wimperntusche [vimpern-toosh-uh]

MECHANIC 69

mashed potatoes der Kartoffelbrei [kart*o*ffel-bry]
massage eine Massage [mass*a*h-djuh]
mast der Mast [masst]
mat die Matte [mat-uh]
match: a box of matches eine Schachtel Streichhölzer [sha*k*-tel shtrysh-hurltser]
 soccer match ein Fußballspiel [fooss-bal-shpeel]
material das Material [ma-tay-ree-*a*hl]
matter: it doesn't matter das macht nichts [dass mah*k*t nix]
 what's the matter? was ist los? [vass ist lohss]
mattress die Matratze [ma-tr*a*ts-uh]
mature reif [rife]
maximum maximal [maxi-m*a*hl]
 (noun) das Maximum [maxim*oo*m]
 that's our maximum offer das ist unser höchstes Angebot [... *oo*nz-er hurrk-stess an-gheh-boht]
May Mai [my]
may: may I have...? darf ich ... haben [... ish ... hah-ben]
 may I...? darf ich ...?
maybe vielleicht [fee-ly*s*ht]
mayonnaise die Mayonnaise [my-on-ay-zuh]
me mich [mish]
 with/from me mit/von mir [... fon meer]
 give it to me geben Sie es mir
 it was me ich war es [ish var ess]
meal das Essen
mean: what does this mean? was heißt das? [vass hysst dass]
 by all means! aber natürlich [ah-ber nat*öö*r-lish]
measles die Masern [mah-zern]
 German measles die Röteln [rurr-teln]
measurements die Maße [mahss-uh]
meat das Fleisch [flysh]
mechanic: is there a mechanic here? gibt es hier einen Mechaniker? [gheept ess heer ine-en mec*k*-*a*hn-iker]

70 MEDICINE

medicine die Medizin [medi-ts*ee*n]
meet treffen
  pleased to meet you angenehm!
  [an-gheh-naym]
meeting die Besprechung [buh-shpresh-ŏong]
  (conference) die Sitzung [zitsoong]
melon eine Melone [meh-l*oh*-nuh]
member das Mitglied [mit-gleet]
  how do I become a member? wie werde ich
  Mitglied? [vee vair-duh ish mit-gleet]
men die Männer [men-er]
  men's rest room die Herrentoilette
  [heh-ren-twah-lettuh]
mend: can you mend this? können Sie das
  wieder in Ordnung bringen? [kurrnen zee dass
  veeder in ort-noong bring-en]
mention: don't mention it gern geschehen
  [gairn gheh-sh*ay*-en]
menu die Speisekarte [shpy-zuh-kar-tuh]
  may I have the menu, please? kann ich,
  bitte, die Speisekarte haben? [kan ish bittuh
  dee . . . hah-ben]
  see pages 72-73
mess ein Durcheinander [dŏorsh-ine-ander]
message: are there any messages for me?
  hat jemand eine Nachricht für mich
  hinterlassen? [. . . yay-mannt ine-uh
  nah*k*-risht fŏor mish . . .]
  may I leave a message for . . .? kann ich eine
  Nachricht für . . . hinterlassen?
meter der Meter [may-ter]
  » *TRAVEL TIP: 1 meter = 39.37 in. = 1.09 yd*
midday der Mittag [mittahg]
middle die Mitte [mittuh]
  in the middle in der Mitte [in dair mittuh]
midnight Mitternacht [mitter-nah*k*t]
might: I might be wrong vielleicht hab' ich
  unrecht [fee-lysht hab ish ŏon-resht]
  he might have gone er ist vielleicht schon
  gegangen [air ist fee-lysht shohn
  gheh-g*a*ng-en]
migraine die Migräne [mee-gr*ai*n-uh]

MISTAKE 71

mild mild [milt]
mile die Meile [my-luh]
» *TRAVEL TIP: conversion:* $\frac{miles}{5} \times 8 =$ *kilometers*

miles	½	1	3	5	10	50	100
kilometers	0.8	1.6	4.8	8	16	80	160

milk die Milch [milsh]
 a glass of milk ein Glas Milch
milkshake ein Milchmixgetränk
 [milsh-mix-gheh-trenk]
millimeter der Millimeter [–mayter]
mind: I've changed my mind ich habe es mir
 anders überlegt [ish hah-buh ess meer anders
 ōōberlaygt]
 I don't mind das macht mir nichts aus [dass
 mahkt meer nix ōwss]
 do you mind if I . . .? macht es Ihnen etwas
 aus, wenn ich . . .? [mahkt ess ee-nen etvass
 ōwss ven ish . . .]
 never mind macht nichts [mahkt nix]
mine mein [mine]
mineral water das Mineralwasser
 [minerahl-vasser]
minimum das Minimum [minimōōm]
minus minus [mee-nooss]
minute die Minute [minoo-tuh]
 he'll be here in a minute er kommt gleich
 [air . . . glysh]
 just a minute einen Moment, bitte [ine-en
 moh-ment bittuh]
mirror der Spiegel [shpee-ghel]
Miss Fräulein [froy-line]
miss: I miss you du fehlst mir [doo faylst meer]
 he's missing er ist verschwunden [air ist
 fair-shvoonden]
 there's a . . . missing da fehlt ein . . . [dah
 faylt ine . . .]
mist der Nebel [naybel]
mistake ein Fehler [fayler]
 I think you've made a mistake ich glaube,
 Sie haben einen Fehler begangen [ish glow-buh
 zee hah-ben ine-en fayler buh-gang-en]

MENU

Vorspeisen: Appetizers
Geräucherter Aal *smoked eel*
Königspastete *chicken-a-la-king*
Krabbencocktail: *shrimp cocktail*
Meefischli *small fried fish from River Main*
Weinbergschnecken *snails*

Suppen: Soups
Blumenkohlsuppe *cream of cauliflower*
Brotsuppe *(Black Forest) bread soup*
Flädlesuppe *(Swabia) consommé with pancake strips*
Hühnerbrühe *chicken broth*
Klößchensuppe *clear soup with dumplings*
Kraftbrühe mit Ei *consommé with a raw egg*
Ochsenschwanzsuppe *oxtail soup*
Tagessuppe *soup of the day*

Vom Rind: Beef
Bouletten *(Berlin) meatballs*
Deutsches Beefsteak *hamburger patty*
Rinderbraten *pot roast*
Rinderfilet *steak*
Rindsrouladen *stuffed beef rolls*
Rostbraten *(Swabia) steak with onions*
Sauerbraten *marinaded pot roast*

Vom Schwein: Pork
Eisbein *knuckles of pork*
Karbonade *(Berlin) roast ribs of pork*
Kotelett *chops*
Leberkäse *(South Germany) baked pork and beef loaf*
Schweinebraten *roast pork*
Schweineschnitzel *pork fillets*

Vom Kalb: Veal
Gefüllte Kalbsbrust *veal roll*
Kalbshaxe *leg of veal*
Jägerschnitzel *veal with mushrooms*
Wienerschnitzel *veal in breadcrumbs*
Zigeunerschnitzel *veal with peppers and relishes*

SPEISEKARTE

Wild: Game
Rehbraten *roast venison*
Wildschweinsteak *wild boar steak*

Fischgerichte: Fish
Forelle Müllerin *trout with butter and lemon*
Karpfen blau *boiled blue carp*
Matjesheringe *pickled herrings*

Other meats
Bockwurst *large Frankfurter sausage*
Bratwurst *grilled pork sausage*
Halbes Hähnchen *half a (roast) chicken*

Spezialitäten: Specialities
Himmel und Erde *(Rhineland) potatoes and apple sauce with black pudding*
Kohl und Pinkel *(Bremen) cabbage and potatoes with sausages and smoked meat*
Labskaus *(Hamburg) potatoes mixed with pieces of fish and meat*
Weißwürste mit Senf *(Munich) white sausages and sweet mustard*

Beilagen: Side dishes
Blumenkohl *cauliflower*; Bratkartoffeln *roast potatoes*; Erbsen *peas*; gemischter Salat *mixed salad*; Gemüseplatte *mixed vegetables*; Kartoffelpüree *mashed potatoes*; Klöße, Knödel *dumplings*; Pommes Frites *French fried potatoes*; Rosenkohl *Brussels sprouts*; Salzkartoffel *boiled potatoes*; Sauerkraut *pickled cabbage*; Spargel *asparagus*; Spätzle *homemade noodles*

Nachspeisen: Desserts
Gemischtes Eis mit Sahne *assorted ice creams with whipped cream*
Eisbecher *parfait*
Obstsalat *fruit salad*
Rote Grütze *(North Germany) fruit blancmange*
Käseplatte *cheeseboard*
Schwarzwälderkirschtorte *Black Forest gateau*

74 MISUNDERSTANDING

misunderstanding ein Mißverständnis [miss-fair-shtent-niss]
modern modern [mod*ai*rn]
Monday Montag [mohn-tahg]
money das Geld [gelt]
  I've lost my money ich habe mein Geld verloren [ish hah-buh mine gelt fair-l*o*r-ren]
  no money kein Geld [kine gelt]
month der Monat [moh-naht]
moon der Mond [mohnt]
moped das Moped
more mehr [mair]
  may I have some more? kann ich noch etwas haben? [kan ish no*k* etvass hah-ben]
  more wine, please noch etwas Wein, bitte [no*k* etvass vine bittuh]
  no more nicht mehr [nisht mair]
  more comfortable bequemer [buh-kv*a*y-mer]
  more than mehr als [mair alts]
morning der Morgen [mor-ghen]
  this morning heute morgen [hoy-tuh ...]
  good morning guten Morgen [gooten ...]
  in the morning morgens [morghenz]
most: I like it/you most das gefällt/Sie gefallen mir am besten [... gheh-f*e*llt/zee gheh-f*a*l-en meer ...]
  most of the time/most of the people meistens/die meisten Leute [my-stenz/dee my-sten loy-tuh]
mother: my mother meine Mutter [mine-uh m*oo*ter]
motor der Motor
motorboat das Motorboot [–boht]
motorcycle das Motorrad [–raht]
motorcyclist der Motorradfahrer [mot*o*r-raht-fah-rer]
motorist der Autofahrer [ōw-toh-fah-rer]
mountain der Berg [bairk]
mountaineer ein Bergsteiger [bairk-shtyger]
mountaineering das Bergsteigen [bairk-shtygen]
mouse die Maus [mōwss]

NAKED 75

mouth der Mund [moont]
move: don't move bewegen Sie sich nicht! [buh-vay-ghen zee zish nisht]
 could you move your car? könnten Sie Ihren Wagen wegfahren? [kurrnten zee ee-ren vah-ghen vek-fahren]
movie ein Film
 let's go to the movies gehen wir ins Kino [gay-en veer ints kee-noh]
movie camera die Filmkamera
movie theater das Kino [kee-noh]
Mr. Herr [hair]
Mrs. Frau [frow]
Ms Frau [frow]
much viel [feel]
 much better/much more viel besser/viel mehr [feel . . ./feel mair]
 not much nicht viel [nisht feel]
mug: I've been mugged ich bin überfallen worden [ish bin ööber-fal-en vorden]
muggy schwül [shvööl]
muscle der Muskel [mooss-kel]
museum das Museum [moo-zay-oom]
mushroom der Pilz [pillts]
music die Musik [moozeek]
must: I must have . . . ich muß . . . haben [ish mooss . . . hah-ben]
 I must not eat . . . ich darf . . . nicht essen [ish darf . . . nisht . . .]
 you must do it Sie müssen es tun [zee möössen ess toon]
mustache der Schnurrbart [shnoor-bart]
mustard der Senf [zenf]
MwSt = Mehrwertsteuer *sales tax*
my mein [mine]
nail *(finger, wood)* der Nagel [nah-ghel]
nail clippers der Nagelzwicker [–tsvicker]
nail file die Nagelfeile [–fy-luh]
nail polish der Nagellack [–lack]
nail scissors die Nagelschere [–shay-ruh]
naked nackt

76 NAME

name der Name [nah-muh]
  my name is ... ich heiße ... [ish hyss-uh ...]
  what's your name? wie heißen Sie? [vee hyssen zee]
napkin die Serviette [zair-vee-ettuh]
narrow eng
national national [nats-ee-oh-nahl]
nationality die Nationalität [nats-ee-oh-nahl-ee-tayt]
natural natürlich [nat͞oorlish]
near: is it near? ist es in der Nähe? [ist ess in dair nay-uh]
  near here hier in der Nähe [heer in dair nay-uh]
  do you go near ...? kommen Sie in die Nähe von ...? [... zee in dee nay-uh fon]
  where's the nearest ...? wo ist der (die/das) nächste ...? [voh ist dair (dee/dass) nex-tuh]
nearly fast [fasst]
necessary notwendig [noht-vendish]
  it's not necessary das ist nicht notwendig
neck der Hals [hallts]
necklace die Halskette [hallts-ket-uh]
need: I need a ... ich brauche einen ... [ish brōwk-uh ine-en ...]
needle die Nadel [nah-del]
negotiations die Verhandlungen [fair-hannt-loong-en]
neighbor der Nachbar [nahk-bar]
neither: neither of them keiner von beiden [kine-er fon by-den]
  neither ... nor ... weder ... noch ... [vayder ... nok ...]
  neither do I ich auch nicht [ish ōwk nisht]
nephew: my nephew mein Neffe [mine neffuh]
nervous nervös [nair-vurrs]
net das Netz
net price der Nettopreis [–price]
never niemals [nee-mallts]
new neu [noy]
news die Nachrichten [nahk-rishten]
newspaper eine Zeitung [tsytoong]

NO 77

do you have any American newspapers?
haben Sie amerikanische Zeitungen?
[hah-ben zee am-ay-ree-*k*ah-nish-uh tsytœong-en]
newsstand der Zeitungshändler
[tsytœongs-henntler]
New Year Neujahr [noy-yahr]
New Year's Eve Silvester
Happy New Year! ein gutes neues Jahr! [ine gootes noy-es yahr]
» *TRAVEL TIP: New Year is traditionally celebrated with fireworks and champagne at midnight when people say 'Prosit Neujahr'* [prohst noy-yahr]; *the next day and afterwards they say 'ein gutes neues Jahr'*
next nächster [nexter]
please stop at the next corner halten Sie, bitte, an der nächsten Ecke [. . . zee bittuh an dair nexten eckuh]
see you next year bis nächstes Jahr [bis nextes yahr]
sit next to me setzen Sie sich neben mich [zet-sen zee zish nay-ben mish]
nice schön [shurrn]
(person) nett
nicht berühren do not touch
nicht öffnen do not open
Nichtraucher no smoking
niece: my niece meine Nichte [mine-uh nishtuh]
night die Nacht [nah*k*t]
good night gute Nacht [gootuh nah*k*t]
at night nachts [nah*k*ts]
night club Nachtklub [nah*k*t-klœob]
nightgown das Nachthemd [nah*k*t-hemmt]
nightlife das Nachtleben [nah*k*t-lay-ben]
night porter der Nachtportier [nah*k*t-por-tee-ay]
no nein [nine]
there's no water wir haben kein Wasser [veer hah-ben kine vasser]
no way! auf keinen Fall! [ōwf kine-en fal]

78 NOBODY

nobody niemand [nee-mannt]
   nobody saw it keiner hat es gesehen [kine-er hat ess gheh-z*a*y-en]
noisy laut [l*ō*wt]
   our room's too noisy in unserem Zimmer ist es zu laut [in o͞onzerem tsimmer ist ess tsoo . . .]
none keiner [kine-er]
   none of them keiner von ihnen [kine-er fon ee-nen]
nonsense Quatsch [kvatsh]
normal normal [norm*a*hl]
north der Norden
Norway Norwegen [nor-vay-ghen]
nose die Nase [nah-zuh]
nosebleed das Nasenbluten [nah-zen-bloo-ten]
not nicht [nisht]
   I'm not hungry ich habe keinen Hunger [ish hah-buh kine-en ho͞ong-er]
   not that one das nicht [dass nisht]
   not me ich nicht
   I don't understand ich verstehe das nicht [ish fair-sht*a*y-uh dass nisht]
   he didn't tell me er hat mir das nicht gesagt [air hat meer dass nisht gheh-z*a*hgt]
Notausgang emergency exit
Notbremse emergency brake
nothing nichts [nix]
November November
now jetzt [yetst]
nowhere nirgends [neer-ghents]
nudist der FKK-Anhänger [eff-ka-ka-an-heng-er]
   nudist beach der FKK-Strand [–shtrannt]
nuisance: it's a nuisance das ist ärgerlich [dass ist air-guh-lish]
   this man's being a nuisance der Mann belästigt mich [. . . buh-*l*est-isht mish]
numb taub [t*ō*wp]
number die Zahl [tsahl]
nurse die Krankenschwester [kranken-shvester]
   (male) der Pfleger [pflay-gher]

ON 79

nursery *(at airport, etc.)* die Kinderkrippe [kinder-krippuh]
nut die Nuß [nooss]
  (for bolt) die (Schrauben)mutter [shrōwben-mooter]
oar das Ruder [rooder]
obligatory obligatorisch [oh-bleegato̱r-rish]
obviously offensichtlich [off-en-zisht-lish]
occasionally gelegentlich [gheh-la̱y-ghent-lish]
occupied besetzt [buh-ze̱tst]
  is this seat occupied? sitzt hier jemand? [zitst heer yay-mannt]
o'clock *see* **time**
October Oktober
odd *(number)* ungerade [oon-gheh-rah-duh]
  (strange) seltsam [ze̱lt-zahm]
odometer der Kilometerzähler [kilo-mayter-tsayler]
of von [fon]
off: it just came off es ist einfach abgegangen [... ine-fahk app-gheh-gang-en]
  10% off 10% Ermäßigung [tsayn proh-tsent air-mace-ee-goong]
office das Büro [booroh]
official *(noun)* der Beamte [buh-am-tuh]
Öffnungszeiten *opening hours*
often oft
oil das Öl [urrl]
  I'm losing oil mein Wagen verliert Öl [mine vah-ghen fair-leert urrl]
  will you change the oil? könnten Sie, bitte, das Öl wechseln? [kurrnten zee bittuh dass urrl vek-seln]
ointment die Salbe [zahl-buh]
OK okay
old alt
  how old are you? wie alt sind Sie? [vee alt zinnt zee]
omelet ein Omelett(e) [omuh-lett(uh)]
on auf [ōwf]
  I haven't got it on me ich habe es nicht bei mir [ish hah-buh ess nisht by meer]

80 ONCE

on Friday am Freitag [am fry-tahg]
on television im Fernsehen [im fairn-zay-en]
once einmal [ine-mahl]
  at once sofort [zoh-fort]
one ein [ine]
  (number) eins [ine-ts]
  the red one der (die/das) rote [dair (dee/dass) roh-tuh]
one-way: a one-way ticket to... eine einfache Fahrkarte nach... [ine-uh ine-fah*k*-uh far-kar-tuh nah*k*]
onion die Zwiebel [tsvee-bel]
only nur [noor]
  he is the only one er ist der einzige [air ist dair ine-tsig-uh]
open *(adjective)* offen
  (store, etc.) geöffnet [geh-*u*rrf-net]
  I can't open it ich bekomme es nicht auf [ish buh-kommuh ess nisht ōwf]
  when do you open? wann machen Sie auf? [van mah*k*en zee ōwf]
opera die Oper [oh-per]
operation die Operation [oh-per-ats-ee-*o*hn]
  will I need an operation? muß ich operiert werden? [m*oo*ss ish oh-per-*ee*rt vairden]
operator *(tel)* die Vermittlung [fair-m*i*tt-l*oo*ng]
opposite: opposite the hotel gegenüber vom Hotel [gay-ghen-ōōber fom...]
optician der Optiker
or oder [oh-der]
orange die Orange [or*o*nj-uh]
  orange juice der Orangensaft [oronjen-zafft]
order: could we order now? könnten wir jetzt bestellen? [kurrnten veer yetst buh-sht*e*llen]
  thank you, we've already ordered danke, wir haben schon bestellt [dankuh veer hah-ben shohn buh-sht*e*llt]
other: the other one der (die, das) andere [dair (dee, dass) an-der-uh]
  do you have any others? haben Sie irgendwelche anderen? [hah-ben zee eerghent-velsh-uh an-der-en]

OYSTER 81

otherwise sonst [zonnst]
ought: I ought to go ich sollte gehen [ish zolltuh gay-en]
ounce die Unze [oonts-uh]
» *TRAVEL TIP: 1 ounce = 28.35 grams*
our unser [oon-zer]
   that's ours das ist unseres [. . . oon-zer-es]
out: we're out of gas uns ist das Benzin ausgegangen [oonts ist dass ben-tseen ōwss-gheh-gang-en]
   get out! raus! [rōwss]
outdoors im Freien [im fry-en]
outlet die Steckdose [shteck-doh-zuh]
   outlet for shavers eine Steckdose für Rasierapparate [. . . för ra-zeer-app-a-rah-tuh]
outside: may we sit outside? können wir draußen sitzen? [kurrnen veer dröwssen zitsen]
over: over here/there hier/dort drüben [heer/dort drōōben]
   over 40 über vierzig [ōōber feer-tsish]
   it's all over es ist aus [ess ist ōwss]
overboard: man overboard! Mann über Bord! [man ōōber bort]
overcharge: you've overcharged me Sie haben mir zu viel berechnet [zee hah-ben meer tsoo feel buh-resh-net]
overcooked zu lange gekocht [tsoo lang-uh gheh-kokt]
overexposed überbelichtet [ōōber-buh-likt-et]
overnight *(stay, travel)* über Nacht [ōōber nahkt]
oversleep verschlafen [fair-shlah-fen]
   I overslept ich habe verschlafen [ish hah-buh fair-shlah-fen]
owe: what do I owe you? was bin ich Ihnen schuldig? [vass bin ish ee-nen shooldish]
own *(adjective)* eigen [eye-ghen]
   my own car mein eigenes Auto
   I'm on my own ich bin allein hier [ish bin al-ine heer]
owner der Eigentümer [eye-ghen-tōōmer]
oxygen der Sauerstoff [zōw-er-shtoff]
oyster die Auster [ōw-ster]

82 PACK

pack: I haven't packed yet ich habe noch nicht gepackt [ish hah-buh no*k* nisht gheh-p*a*ckt]
package das Paket [pa-kayt]
package tour die Pauschalreise [pōw-sh*a*hl-ry-zuh]
page *(of book)* die Seite [zy-tuh]
 could you page him? können Sie ihn ausrufen lassen? [kurrnen zee een ōwss-roofen . . .]
pain der Schmerz [shmairts]
 I've got a pain in my . . . mir tut mein . . . weh [meer toot mine . . . vay]
painkiller ein schmerzstillendes Mittel [schmairts-shtill-end-es . . .]
painting das Gemälde [gheh-m*e*hl-duh]
pair das Paar [par]
pajamas der Schlafanzug [shlahf-an-tsoog]
pale blaß [blass]
pancake der Pfannkuchen [pfan-koo*k*en]
panties das Höschen [hurrs-shen]
pants die Hose [hoh-zuh]
pantyhose die Strumpfhose [shtr*oo*mpf-hoh-zuh]
paper das Papier [pa-peer]
 (newspaper) die Zeitung [tsytœng]
pardon me? *(didn't understand)* wie bitte? [vee bittuh]
 I beg your pardon *(sorry)* Entschuldigung [ent-sh*oo*ld-ee-gœng]
parents: my parents meine Eltern
park der Park
 where can I park? wo kann ich parken? [voh . . .]
Parken nur mit Parkscheibe parking token required *(attached to windshield, indicates when parking commenced)*
Parken verboten no parking
parking lights die Standlichter [shtannt-lishter]
parking lot der Parkplatz
Parkplatz parking lot

PEN PAL 83

part ein Teil [ine tile]
partner der Partner
party *(group)* die Gruppe [groop-uh]
  (travel) die Gesellschaft [gheh-zell-shafft]
  (celebration) die Party
  I'm with the ... party ich bin mit
  der ... Gruppe hier
pass *(mountain)* der Paß [pas]
  (in car) überholen [oober-hoh-len]
passable *(road)* passierbar [pas-eer-bar]
passenger ein Reisender [ry-zender]
  (on ship, plane) ein Passagier [pass-ajeer]
passerby ein Passant
passport der Paß [pas]
past: in the past früher [froo-er]
pastry das Gebäck [gheh-beck]
path der Weg [vayg]
patient *(in hospital)* der Patient [pats-ee-ent]
  be patient Geduld! [gheh-doolt]
pattern das Muster [mooster]
pay bezahlen [buh-tsahlen]
  may I pay, please? ich möchte gerne zahlen
  [ish murrshtuh gairn-uh tsahlen]
pay phone eine Telefonzelle [–tselluh]
peas Erbsen [erp-sen]
peace der Frieden [free-den]
peach ein Pfirsich [pfeer-zish]
peanuts Erdnüsse [airt-nooss-uh]
pear eine Birne [beer-nuh]
pebble ein Kieselstein [kee-zel-shtine]
pedal das Pedal [pay-dahl]
pedestrian ein Fußgänger [fooss-genger]
peg der Stift [shtift]
  (for tent) der Hering [hay-ring]
  (mountaineering) der Haken [hah-ken]
pelvis das Becken
pen der Kugelschreiber [kooghel-shryber]
  have you got a pen? haben Sie etwas zum
  Schreiben? [hah-ben zee etvass tsoom shryben]
pencil ein Bleistift [bly-shtift]
penicillin das Penizillin [pen-its-illeen]
pen pal ein Brieffreund [breef-froynt]

84 PEOPLE

people die Leute [loy-tuh]
   the German people die Deutschen [doyt-shen]
pepper der Pfeffer
   green/red pepper der grüne/rote Paprika [grōōnuh/roh-tuh ...]
peppermint das Pfefferminz
per: per night/week/person pro Nacht/Woche/Person [proh nah*k*t/*v*o*k*-uh/pair-*z*ohn]
percent Prozent [proh-ts*e*nt]
perfect perfekt [pair-f*e*kt]
   the perfect vacation der ideale Urlaub [dair ee-day-ahl-uh oorlōwp]
perfume das Parfüm [parfōōm]
perhaps vielleicht [fee-lysht]
period der Zeitraum [tsyt-rōwm]
   (woman's) die Periode [pay-ree-oh-duh]
permanent wave die Dauerwelle [dōw-er-vell-uh]
permit *(noun)* die Genehmigung [gheh-n*a*y-mig*œ*ng] see entry
person die Person [pair-*z*ohn]
   in person persönlich [pair-*zu*rrn-lish]
pharmacy eine Apotheke [apo-t*a*y-kuh]
» *TRAVEL TIP: pharmacies display a notice about night service (Nachtdienst) and Sunday service (Sonntagsdienst)*
phone *see* **telephone**
photograph die Fotografie [foto-gra-f*ee*]
   would you take a photograph of us? würden Sie ein Bild von uns machen? [v*ōō*rden zee ine bilt fon *œ*nts mah-*k*en]
piano das Klavier [kla-v*ee*r]
pickpocket der Taschendieb [tashen-deep]
pick up *(shirts, etc.)* abholen [app-hoh-len]
   I want to pick up ... ich möchte ... abholen [ish murrshtuh ...]
   would you pick me up? würden Sie mich abholen? [v*ōō*rden zee mish ...]
picture ein Bild [bilt]
pie die Pastete [pas-t*a*y-tuh]
   (dessert) der Obstkuchen [ohpst-koo*k*en]

PLASTIC 85

apple pie der Apfelkuchen [apfel-koo*k*en]
piece das Stück [sht‾oo‾ck]
 a piece of cheese ein Stück Käse [ine sht‾oo‾ck kay-zuh]
pig das Schwein [shvine]
pigeon die Taube [tōw-buh]
pileup die Massenkarambolage [massen-karambo-*la*h-juh]
pill eine Tablette [tab-l*e*ttuh]
 do you take the pill? nimmst du die Pille? [. . . pill-uh]
pillow das Kissen
pin die (Steck)nadel [(shteck)nah-del]
pineapple eine Ananas
pink *(adjective)* rosa
pint
» *TRAVEL TIP: 1 pint = 0.47 liters*
pipe die Pfeife [pfy-fuh]
 (sink, etc.) das Rohr [ror]
pipe tobacco der Pfeifentabak [pfy-fen-tabak]
pity: it's a pity das ist schade [dass ist shah-duh]
Pkw [pay-ka-vay] = ***Personenkraftwagen***
 (private) automobile
place der Platz
 (town) der Ort
 is this place taken? ist hier besetzt? [ist heer buh-z*e*tst]
 do you know any good places to go? wissen Sie, wo man hingehen könnte? [vissen zee voh man hin-gay-en kurrntuh]
plain *(food)* (gut)bürgerlich [(goot)b‾oo‾r-gher-lish]
 (not patterned) einfarbig [ine-farbish]
plan der Plan [plahn]
plane das Flugzeug [floog-tsoyg]
plant die Pflanze [pflannts-uh]
 (factory) das Werk [vairk]
 (equipment) die Anlagen [an-läh-ghen]
plaster cast der Gips [ghips]
plastic Plastik
 plastic bag eine Plastiktüte [–t‾oo‾t-uh]

plate der Teller
platform der Bahnsteig [bahn-shtyg]
play *(verb)* spielen [shpeelen]
　(theater) ein Theaterstück [tay-ah-ter-shtöock]
pleasant angenehm
please: could you please ...? könnten Sie, bitte, ...? [kurrnten zee bittuh]
　(yes) please ja, bitte [yah bittuh]
pleasure das Vergnügen [fair-guh-nōō-ghen]
　my pleasure gern geschehen [gairn gheh-shay-en]
plenty: plenty of ... viel ... [feel]
　thank you, that's plenty danke, das reicht [dan-kuh dass rysht]
pliers eine Zange [tsang-uh]
plug *(elec.)* der Stecker [shtecker]
　(car) die Zündkerze [tsōont-kairts-uh]
　(bathroom) der Stöpsel [shturrp-sel]
plum eine Pflaume [pflōwm-uh]
plus plus [plœss]
p.m. nachmittags [nahk-mittahgs]
pneumonia die Lungenentzündung [loong-en-ent-tsōondœng]
poached egg ein pochiertes Ei [posheertes eye]
pocket die Tasche [tash-uh]
pocketbook die Handtasche [hannt-tash-uh]
pocketknife das Taschenmesser [tashen–]
point: could you point to it? könnten Sie darauf deuten? [kurrnten zee darōwf doyten]
　four point six vier komma sechs [feer ... zex]
points *(car)* die Unterbrecherkontakte [œnter-bresher-kontakt-uh]
police die Polizei [polits-eye]
　get the police holen Sie die Polizei [hoh-len zee dee ...]
» *TRAVEL TIP:* dial 211
policeman der Polizist [polits-ist]
police station die (Polizei)wache [... vahk-uh]
polish *(noun: shoes)* die Schuhcreme [shoo-kray-muh]

POUR 87

could you have my shoes polished?
könnten Sie meine Schuhe putzen lassen?
[kurrnten zee mine-uh shoo-uh pootsen lassen]
polite höflich [hurrf-lish]
politics die Politik [poli-teek]
polluted verschmutzt [fair-shmootst]
pool *(swimming)* das Schwimmbad
[shvimm-baht]
poor: I'm very poor ich bin sehr arm [ish bin zair . . .]
 poor quality schlechte Qualität [shlekt-uh kval-ee-tayt]
popular beliebt [buh-leept]
population die Bevölkerung
[buh-furlk-kuh-roong]
pork das Schweinefleisch [shvine-uh-flysh]
port *(harbor)* der Hafen [hah-fen]
 (opp. starboard) Backbord [–bort]
 (drink) der Portwein [–vine]
porter der Gepäckträger [gheh-peck-tray-gher]
portrait das Porträt [por-tray]
Portugal Portugal [port-oo-gahl]
possible möglich [murr-glish]
 could you possibly . . .? könnten Sie
 eventuell . . .? [kurrnten zee ay-vent-oo-el]
postcard die Postkarte [posst-kar-tuh]
post office das Postamt [posst-amt]
» *TRAVEL TIP: post offices generally open from 8:00–6:00 Monday to Friday and 8:00 to 12:00 on Saturdays*
potato die Kartoffel
potato chips Chips
pottery die Töpferei [turrpfer-eye]
 (pots) die Töpferwaren [turrpfer-vah-ren]
 (glazed) die Keramik [kay-rah-mik]
pound das Pfund [pfoont]
» *TRAVEL TIP: conversion:* $\frac{pounds}{11} \times 5 = kilos$

pounds	1	3	5	6	7	8	9
kilos	0.45	1.4	2.3	2.7	3.2	3.6	4.1

a German Pfund = 500 grams
pour: it's pouring es gießt [ess geest]

88 POWDER

powder das Pulver [pool-ver]
  (face) der Puder [poo-der]
power failure der Stromausfall [shtrohm-owss-fal]
prefer: I prefer this one das gefällt mir besser [... gheh-fe̊llt meer ...]
  I'd prefer to ... ich würde lieber ... [ish voor-duh lee-ber]
  I'd prefer a ... ich hätte lieber ein ... [ish het-uh lee-ber ine ...]
pregnant schwanger [shvang-er]
prescription das Rezept [rets-e̊pt]
present: at present zur Zeit [tsoor tsite]
  present company excepted Anwesende ausgeschlossen [anvay-zend-uh owss-gheh-shlossen]
  here's a present for you ein Geschenk für Sie [ine gheh-she̊nk foor zee]
president der Präsident [pray-zide̊nt]
press: could you press these? könnten Sie sie bügeln? [kurrnten zee zee boo-gheln]
pretty hübsch [hoopsh]
  it's pretty good es ist ganz gut [... gants goot]
price der Preis [price]
priest der Priester [preester]
print *(photo)* ein Abzug [app-tsoog]
printed matter Drucksache [droock-zahk-uh]
prison das Gefängnis [gheh-fe̊ngnis]
private privat [pree-våht]
probably wahrscheinlich [vahr-shi̊ne-lish]
problem das Problem [prob-låym]
product das Produkt [prodoockt]
profit der Gewinn [gheh-vi̊nn]
promise: do you promise? versprechen Sie es? [fair-shpre̊shen zee ess]
  I promise ehrlich! [åir-lish]
pronounce: how do you pronounce it? wie spricht man das aus? [vee shprisht man dass owss]
properly richtig [ri̊sh-tish]
property das Eigentum [eye-ghen-toom]
  (land) der Besitz [buh-zi̊ts]

PUT 89

prostitute die Prostituierte [prostit-oo-*ee*r-tuh]
protect schützen [sh**oo**tsen]
Protestant evangelisch [ay-van-g*a*y-lish]
proud stolz [shtolts]
prove: I can prove it ich kann es beweisen [ish kan ess buh-v*i*se-en]
public: the public die Öffentlichkeit [urrfent-lish-kite]
 public holiday gesetzlicher Feiertag [gheh-zets-lisher fire-tahg]
» *TRAVEL TIP: public holidays are:*
 New Year's Day *Neujahr*
 Good Friday *Karfreitag*
 Easter Monday *Ostermontag*
 May Day *Erster Mai*
 Ascension Day *Christi Himmelfahrt*
 Whit Monday (Pentecost) *Pfingstmontag*
 National Unity Day *Tag der deutschen Einheit (June 17)*
 Day of Prayer and Repentance *Buß- und Bettag (mid Nov.)*
 Christmas Day *1. (erster) Weihnachtsfeiertag*
 the day after Christmas *2. (zweiter) Weihnachtsfeiertag;*
 in the mainly Catholic parts there is also:
 Epiphany *Dreikönige*
 Corpus Christi *Fronleichnam*
 Assumption *Mariä Himmelfahrt*
pull *(verb)* ziehen [tsee-en]
 he pulled out in front of me er ist vor mir ausgeschert [air ist for meer **ow**ss-gheh-shayrt]
pump die Pumpe [p**oo**m-puh]
punctual pünktlich [p**oo**nkt-lish]
pure rein [rine]
purple lila [lee-lah]
purse das Portemonnaie [port-mon-*a*y]
 (handbag) die Handtasche [hannt-tash-uh]
push *(verb)* schieben [sheeben]
put: where can I put...? wo kann ich... hintun? [voh kan ish ... hintoon]

90 QUALITY

where have you put it? wo haben Sie es hingetan? [voh hah-ben zee es hin-gheh-tahn]
  put it here bitte hierhin [bittuh heer-hin]
quality die Qualität [kval-ee-tayt]
quarantine die Quarantäne [kvar-an-tayn-uh]
quart
  »TRAVEL TIP: 1 quart = 0.95 liters
quarter ein Viertel [feer-tel]
  a quarter of an hour eine Viertelstunde [ine-uh feer-tel shtoon-duh]
quay der Kai [kye]
question die Frage [frah-guh]
quick schnell [shnel]
  that was quick das ging schnell
quiet ruhig [roo-ish]
  (not noisy) still [shtill]
quite ganz [gants]
  quite a lot ziemlich viel [tseem-lish feel]
race das Rennen
radiator der Kühler [kooler]
  (heater) der Heizkörper [hites-kurr-per]
radio das Radio [rah-dee-oh]
Radweg bicycle path
rail: by rail per Bahn [pair . . .]
railroad crossing der Bahnübergang [bahn-oober-gang]
rain der Regen [ray-ghen]
  it's raining es regnet [ess rayg-net]
rain boots Gummistiefel [goomee-shteefel]
raincoat der Regenmantel
rape die Vergewaltigung [fair-gheh-val-tigoong]
rare selten [z–]
  (steak) blutig [bloo-tish]
raspberries Himbeeren [him-bair-en]
rat die Ratte [rat-uh]
rather: I'd rather sit here ich würde lieber hier sitzen [ish voor-duh lee-ber heer zitsen]
  I'd rather have a . . . ich hätte lieber ein . . . [ish het-uh lee-ber ine]
  I'd rather not lieber nicht! [lee-ber nisht]
Rauchen verboten no smoking
Raucher smoking compartment

REGISTERED 91

raw roh
razor der Rasierapparat [ra-zeer–]
razor blades Rasierklingen
read: you read it lesen Sie es [lay-zen zee ess]
  something to read etwas zu lesen [etvass tsoo...]
ready: when will it be ready? wann ist es fertig [van ist ess fair-tish]
  I'm not ready yet ich bin noch nicht fertig [ish bin nok nisht...]
real *(genuine)* echt [esht]
really wirklich [veerk-lish]
rearview mirror der Rückspiegel [rōōck-shpee-ghel]
reasonable vernünftig [fair-nōōnf-tish]
receipt die Quittung [kvit-oong]
  may I have a receipt, please? kann ich, bitte, eine Quittung haben? [kan ish bittuh ine-uh... hah-ben]
recently kürzlich [kōōrts-lish]
reception *(hotel)* der Empfang
  at reception am Empfang
receptionist der Empfangschef
  (lady) die Empfangsdame [–dah-muh]
recipe das Rezept [rets-ept]
recommend: can you recommend...? können Sie... empfehlen? [kurrnen zee... emp-fay-len]
record *(music)* die Platte [plat-uh]
red rot [roht]
reduction *(in price)* die Ermäßigung [air-mace-ee-goong]
refrigerator der Kühlschrank [kōōl-shrank]
refuse: I refuse ich weigere mich [ish vy-guh-ruh mish]
region das Gebiet [gheh-beet]
  in this region in diesem Gebiet [in dee-zem...]
registered: I want to send it registered ich möchte das per Einschreiben schicken [ish murrshtuh dass pair ine-shryben shicken]

92 REGRET

regret das Bedauern [buh-dōwern]
  I have no regrets ich bereue nichts [ish buh-roy-uh nix]
relax: I just want to relax ich möchte mich nur entspannen [ish murrshtuh mish noor ent-shpannen]
  relax! ganz ruhig! [gants roo-ish]
remember: don't you remember? wissen Sie das nicht mehr? [vissen zee dass nisht mair]
  I'll always remember ich werde es nie vergessen [ish vair-duh ess nee fair-ghessen]
  something to remember you by ein Andenken an dich [ine ... dish]
rent: can I rent a car/boat/bicycle? kann ich ein Auto/Boot/Fahrrad mieten? [... meeten]
repair: can you repair it? können Ses reparieren? [kurrnen zee ess rep-a-ree-ren]
repeat: could you repeat that? könnten Sie das wiederholen? [kurrnten zee dass veeder-hole-en]
reputation der Ruf [roof]
rescue *(verb)* retten
reservation die Reservierung [rez-air-vee-roong]
  I want to make a reservation for ... *(hotel)* ich möchte ein Zimmer für ... bestellen [ish murrshtuh ine tsimmer foor ... buh-shtellen]
  (theater) ich möchte einen Platz reservieren für ... [... ine-en plats rez-air-vee-ren ...]
reserve: can I reserve a seat? kann ich einen Platz reservieren? [kan ish ine-en plats rez-air-vee-ren]
  I'd like to reserve a table for two ich möchte gerne einen Tisch für zwei Personen bestellen [ish murrshtuh gairn-uh ine-en tish foor tsvy pair-zoh-nen buh-shtellen]
  YOU MAY THEN HEAR ...
  wie war der Name, bitte? *what name, please?*
  für wann, bitte? *for what time?*
responsible verantwortlich [fair-ant-vort-lish]

ROAD 93

rest: I've come here for a rest ich bin hier, um mal auszuspannen [ish bin heer om mal ōwss-tsoo-shpannen]
   (remainder) der Rest
restaurant ein Restaurant [–rong]
rest room die Toilette [twa-lettuh]
   where is the rest room? wo ist die Toilette? [voh ist dee . . .]
   public rest room öffentliche Toilette [urrfent-lish-uh twa-lettuh]
» *TRAVEL TIP: there are not very many public rest rooms in Germany – try the railroad station; the attitude towards using a cafe, etc. is the same as in America*
retired pensioniert [pen-zee-oh-neert]
reverse gear der Rückwärtsgang [rōck-vairts–]
rheumatism der Rheumatismus [roy-ma-ti*s*mooss]
rib eine Rippe [rip-uh]
rice der Reis [rice]
rich reich [rysh]
   (food) schwer [shvair]
ride: do you want a ride? kann ich Sie mitnehmen? [kan ish zee m*i*t-nay-men]
   can you give me a ride? könnten Sie mich mitnehmen? [kurrnten . . .]
ridiculous lächerlich [lesh-er-lish]
right: that's right das stimmt [dass shtimmt]
   you're right Sie haben recht [zee hah-ben resht]
   on the right rechts [reshts]
   right here genau hier [gheh-nōw heer]
   right now *(at the moment)* moment*a*n
   (immediately) sofort [zohfort]
ring *(on finger)* der Ring
ripe reif [rife]
rip-off: it's a rip-off das ist Wucher! [dass ist voo*k*-er]
river der Fluß [flooss]
road die Straße [shtrass-uh]
   which is the road to . . . ? wo geht es nach . . . ? [voh gayt ess nah*k* . . .]

94 ROAD HOG

road hog der Verkehrsrowdy [fair-ka*i*rs–]
rob: I've been robbed ich bin bestohlen worden [ish bin buh-sht*o*le-en vorden]
rock der Fels [felts]
   scotch on the rocks Whisky mit Eis [. . . ice]
roll *(bread)* ein Brötchen [brurrt-shen]
Roman Catholic (römisch-) katholisch [(rurr-mish) kat-*o*lish]
romantic romantisch [–tish]
roof das Dach [dah*k*]
room das Zimmer [tsimmer]
   do you have a (single/double) room? haben Sie ein (Einzel/Doppel)zimmer [hah-ben zee ine (ine-tsel/doppel) . . .]
   for one night/for three nights für eine Nacht/für drei Nächte [foor ine-uh nah*k*t/foor dry neshte]
   YOU MAY THEN HEAR . . .
   mit Bad oder ohne? *with or without bath?*
   tut mir leid, wir sind voll ausgebucht/wir haben nichts mehr frei *sorry, we're full*
room service der Zimmerservice [tsimmer-serviss]
rope das Seil [zile]
rose die Rose [roh-zuh]
rough rauh [row]
roughly ungefähr [oon-gheh-fair]
roulette das Roulett(e)
round *(circular)* rund [roont]
round-trip: a round-trip ticket to . . . eine Rückfahrkarte nach . . . [ine-uh rook-far-kar-tuh nah*k*]
route die Strecke [shtreck-uh]
   which is the prettiest/fastest route? welches ist die schönste/schnellste Strecke? [vel-shes ist dee shurrn-stuh/shnel-stuh . . .]
rowboat das Ruderboot [rooder-boht]
rubber der Gummi [goo-mee]
rubber band ein Gummiband [goo-mee-bannt]
rudder das Ruder [rooder]
rude unhöflich [oon-hurrf-lish]
Ruhetag closed all day

ruin die Ruine [roo-een-uh]
rum ein Rum [room]
  rum and Coke Cola mit Rum
run: hurry, run! beeil dich, lauf! [buh-*ile* dish lowf]
  I've run out of gas/money ich habe kein Benzin/Geld mehr [ish hah-buh kine ben-tseen/gelt mair]
Russia Rußland [rooss-lannt]
Sackgasse *dead end*
sad traurig [trow-rish]
safe sicher [zisher]
  will it be safe here? ist es hier sicher? [ist ess heer . . .]
  is it safe to swim here? kann man hier ohne Gefahr schwimmen? [. . . oh-nuh gheh-f*a*hr shvimmen]
safety die Sicherheit [zisher-hite]
safety pin eine Sicherheitsnadel [zisher-hites-nah-del]
sail segeln [zay-gheln]
  may we go sailing? können wir segeln gehen? [kurrnen veer . . . gay-en]
sailor ein Seemann [zay-man]
salad ein Salat [zal-*a*ht]
salami die Salami [z–]
sale: is it for sale? kann man das kaufen? [. . . kow-fen]
sales clerk der Verkäufer [fair-k*oy*-fer]
  (woman) die Verkäuferin
salmon der Lachs [lax]
salt das Salz [zalts]
same der-/die-/dasselbe [dair-/dee-/dass-zelbuh]
  the same to you (danke) gleichfalls [(dankuh) glysh-falts]
sand der Sand [zannt]
sandal die Sandale [zan-d*a*hl-uh]
sandwich ein Sandwich
sanitary napkin die Damenbinde [dah-men-bin-duh]
satisfactory befriedigend [buh-fr*ee*d-ee-ghent]
Saturday Samstag [zamz-tahg]

96 SAUCE

sauce die Soße [zoh-suh]
saucepan der Kochtopf [kok-topf]
saucer der Untertasse [oonter-tass-uh]
sauna die Sauna [zōw-na]
sausage die Wurst [voorst]
save *(life)* retten
say: how do you say ... in German? was heißt ... auf Deutsch? [vass hysst ... ōwf doytsh]
   what did he say? was hat er gesagt? [vass hat air gheh-zahgt]
scarf der Schal [shahl]
   (neckscarf) das Halstuch [hallts-took]
   (headscarf) das Kopftuch
scenery die Landschaft [lannt-shafft]
schedule der Zeitplan [tsite-plahn]
   on/behind schedule pünktlich/verspätet [poonkt-lish/fair-shpaytet]
   (work) **on schedule** programmgemäß [program-gheh-mace]
   behind schedule im Verzug [fair-tsoog]
   scheduled flight der Linienflug [leen-ee-en-floog]
Schlafwagen sleeping car
Schließfächer baggage lockers
Schlußverkauf sale
schnaps ein Schnaps
» *TRAVEL TIP: can be made from practically anything; try North German 'Korn' (grain), Black Forest 'Kirsch' (cherries) or 'Steinhäger' [shtine-hay-gher] (juniper berries)*
school die Schule [shool-uh]
scissors: a pair of scissors eine Schere [ine-uh shay-ruh]
scotch der Whisky [v—]
Scotland Schottland [shott-lannt]
scrambled eggs Rührei [rōōr-eye]
scratch der Kratzer
scream *(verb)* schreien [shry-en]
screw die Schraube [shrōw-buh]
screwdriver ein Schraubenzieher [shrōwben-tsee-er]

SENSITIVE 97

sea das Meer [mayr]
  by the sea am Meer
seafood Meeresfrüchte [mayr-es-fro͞okt-uh]
search die Suche [zook-uh]
search party die Suchmannschaft
  [zook-man-shafft]
seasick: I get seasick ich werde seekrank [ish
  vairduh zay–]
season die Saison [sez-ong]
  in the high/low season in der Hochsaison/
  Nebensaison [in dair hohk–/nay-ben–]
seasoning das Gewürz [geh-vo͞orts]
seat der (Sitz)platz
  is this somebody's seat? sitzt hier jemand?
  [zitst heer yay-mannt]
seat belt der Sicherheitsgurt [zisher-
  hites-goort]
» *TRAVEL TIP: wearing seat belt is compulsory in
  Germany*
seaweed der Tang
second *(adjective)* zweite [tsvy-tuh]
  (time) die Sekunde [zeck-oonduh]
  just a second Moment! [moh-ment]
  second class zweiter Klasse
  [... klass-uh ...]
second hand gebraucht [geh-browkt]
see sehen [zay-en]
  oh, I see ach so! [ahk zoh]
  have you seen ... haben Sie ... gesehen?
  [hah-ben zee ... geh-zay-en]
  may I see the room? kann ich mir das
  Zimmer anschauen? [kan ish meer dass
  tsimmer an-show-en]
seem scheinen [shine-en]
  it seems so so sieht es aus [zoh zeet ess o͞wss]
seldom selten [zelten]
self: self-service Selbstbedienung [zelpst-
  buh-deen-oong]
sell verkaufen [fair-kowfen]
send schicken [shicken]
senior citizen der Rentner
sensitive empfindlich [emp-finnt-lish]

98 SENTIMENTAL

sentimental sentimental
separate getrennt [gheh-trennt]
   I'm separated wir leben getrennt [veer lay-ben . . .]
   can we pay separately? können wir getrennt zahlen? [kurrnen veer . . . tsah-len]
September September [z–]
serious ernst [airnst]
   I'm serious ich meine das ernst [ish my-nuh dass . . .]
   this is serious das ist ernst
   is it serious, doctor? ist es schlimm? [ist ess shlim]
service: the service was excellent/poor der Service war ausgezeichnet/schlecht [dair serviss vahr ōwss-gheh-tsysh-net/shlesht]
service charge Bedienung [buh-dee-noong]
» *TRAVEL TIP: normally included*
service station die Tankstelle (mit Reparaturwerkstatt) [tank-shtelluh (mit rep-a-rah-toor-vairk-shtat)]
several mehrere [mair-uh-ruh]
sexy sexy
shade: in the shade im Schatten [. . . shat-en]
shake schütteln [shoot-eln]
   to shake hands die Hand schütteln [dee hannt . . .]
» *TRAVEL TIP: it is normal to shake hands each time you meet someone and when you leave someone*
shallow seicht [zysht]
shame: what a shame wie schade! [vee shah-duh]
shampoo ein Shampoo(n)
   shampoo and set Waschen und Legen [vashen oont lay-ghen]
share *(room)* teilen [tile-en]
   (table) gemeinsam nehmen [gheh-mine-zahm nay-men]
sharp scharf [sharf]
shave rasieren [ra-zee-ren]
shaving cream der Rasierschaum [ra-zeer-shōwm]

she sie [zee]
  she is sie ist [zee ist]
sheep das Schaf [shahf]
sheet das Leintuch [line-took]
shelf das Regal [ray-gahl]
shell die Schale [shah-luh]
  (on beach) die Muschel [mooshel]
shellfish Meeresfrüchte [mayr-es-frōosh-tuh]
shelter *(noun)* der Unterstand [oonter-shtannt]
sherry ein Sherry
ship das Schiff [shif]
shirt das Hemd [hemmt]
shock *(noun: surprise)* der Schock
  what a shock so ein Schreck! [zoh ine shreck]
  I got an electric shock from the ... ich habe
  von dem ... einen Schlag bekommen [ish
  hah-buh fon daym ... ine-nen shlahg buh–]
shock absorber der Stoßdämpfer [shtohss-dem-pfer]
shoelaces Schnürsenkel [shnōor-zenkel]
shoes die Schuhe [shoo-uh]
» *TRAVEL TIP: shoe sizes:*

women's

US	3½/4	4½	5/5½	6/6½
Germany	35	36	37	38

US	7/7½	8	8½	9/9½
Germany	39	40	41	42

men's

US	7	7½	8	8½/9	9½/10
Germany	39	40	41	42	43

US	10½	11/11½	12	12½/13
Germany	44	45	46	47

shop das Geschäft [gheh-shefft]
  I've some shopping to do ich muß noch ein
  paar Einkäufe erledigen [ish mooss nok ine par
  ine-koy-fuh air-lay-dig-en]
» *TRAVEL TIP: stores generally open from
9:00–6:30; closed Saturday afternoon except the
first Saturday in the month*
shore das Ufer [oofer]
  (sea) der Strand [shtrannt]

100 SHORT

short kurz [koorts]
  I'm three short mir fehlen drei [meer fay-len dry]
shortcut eine Abkürzung [ine-uh app-koorts-oong]
shorts die Shorts
  (underwear) eine Unterhose [oonter-hoh-zuh]
shoulder die Schulter [shoolter]
shout rufen [roofen]
show: please show me bitte zeigen Sie es mir [bittuh tsy-ghen zee ess meer]
shower: with shower mit Dusche [mit doosh-uh]
shrimp eine Garnele [gar-nay-luh]
shrink: it's shrunk es ist eingegangen [ess ist ine-gheh-gang-en]
shut *(verb)* schließen [shlee-sen]
  shut up! halt den Mund! [hallt dayn moont]
shy schüchtern [shoosh-tern]
sick krank
  I feel sick mir ist schlecht [meer ist shlesht]
side die Seite [zy-tuh]
  by the side of the road an der Straße
side street die Nebenstraße [nay-ben-shtrahss-uh]
sidewalk der Gehsteig [gay-shtyg]
sight: out of sight außer Sicht [owsser zisht]
  the sights of ... die Sehenswürdigkeiten von [zay-enz-voord-ish-kite-en fon]
sightseeing tour eine Rundreise [roont-ry-zuh]
  (of town) eine Stadtrundfahrt [shtat-roont-fahrt]
sign *(notice)* das Schild [shilt]
signal: he didn't signal er hat kein Zeichen gegeben [air hat kine tsyshen gheh-gay-ben]
  (turn signal) der Blinker
signature die Unterschrift [oonter-shrift]
silk die Seide [zy-duh]
silly dumm [doomm]
silver das Silber [zilber]
similar ähnlich [ayn-lish]

SLEEPING CAR 101

simple einfach [ine-fah*k*]
since: since last week seit letzter Woche [zite lets-ter vock-uh]
  (because) weil [vile]
sincere aufrichtig [ōwf-rish-tish]
  yours sincerely mit freundlichen Grüßen
sing singen [zing-en]
single: single room ein Einzelzimmer [ine-tsel-tsimmer]
  I'm single ich bin ledig [ish bin lay-dish]
sink: it sank es ist gesunken [ess ist gheh-zoonken]
sir: sir!/excuse me, sir entschuldigen Sie bitte [ent-shooldigen zee bittuh]
  there is no general word for 'sir'; if you know the man's name, say 'Herr Schmidt', etc.
sister: my sister meine Schwester [mine-uh shvester]
sit: may I sit here? kann ich mich hierher setzen? [kan ish mish heer-hair zetsen]
size die Größe [grurr-suh]
ski *(noun)* der Ski [shee]
  (verb) skifahren
  ski boots die Skistiefel [–steefel]
  skiing das Skifahren
  ski lift der Skilift
  ski pants die Skihose [–hoh-zuh]
  ski pole der Skistock [–shtock]
  ski slope/run der Skihang/die Skipiste
  ski wax das Skiwachs [–vax]
skid schleudern [shloy-dern]
skin die Haut [hōwt]
skirt der Rock
sky der Himmel
sled der Schlitten [sh–]
sleep: I can't sleep ich kann nicht schlafen [ish kan nisht shlah-fen]
  YOU MAY HEAR...
  haben Sie gut geschlafen? *did you sleep well?*
sleeping bag der Schlafsack [shlahf-zack]
sleeping car der Schlafwagen [shlahf-vah-ghen]

102 SLEEPING PILL

sleeping pill die Schlaftablette [shlahf-tablettuh]
sleeve der Ärmel [air-mel]
slide *(phot)* das Dia [dee-ah]
slippery glatt
slow langsam [lang-zahm]
   could you speak a little slower? könnten Sie etwas langsamer sprechen? [kurrnten zee etvass lang-zahmer shpreshen]
small klein [kline]
small change das Kleingeld [kline-gelt]
smell: there's a funny smell hier riecht es komisch [heer reesht ess koh-mish]
   it smells es stinkt [ess shtinkt]
smile *(verb)* lächeln [lesh-eln]
smoke *(noun)* der Rauch [rōwk]
   do you smoke? rauchen Sie? [rōwken zee]
   may I smoke? darf ich rauchen?
smooth glatt
snack: can we just have a snack? können wir einen Imbiß bekommen? [kurrnen veer ine-en im-biss buh-kommen]
» *TRAVEL TIP: you will find plenty of indoor and outdoor snackbars called 'Schnellimbiß' or 'Imbißstube' which sell sausages, French fries, etc.*
sneakers Sportschuhe [shport-shoo-uh]
snow *(noun)* der Schnee [shnay]
   it's snowing es schneit [ess shnite]
» *TRAVEL TIP: snow chains (Schneeketten) can be rented from ADAC offices*
so so [zoh]
   not so much nicht so viel [nisht zoh feel]
   so so so la la
soap die Seife [zy-fuh]
sober nüchtern [nōōshtern]
soccer der Fußball [fooss-bal]
sock die Socke [zock-uh]
soda water das Soda(wasser)
soft drink ein alkoholfreies Getränk [al-koh-hole-fry-es geh-trenk]
Sofortreinigung *fast service dry cleaner*

sole die Sohle [zoh-luh]
    could you put new soles on these? könnten Sie diese hier neu besohlen? [kurrnten zee dee-zuh heer noy buh-zoh-len]
    YOU MAY THEN HEAR...
    Leder- oder Gummisohle? *leather or rubber soles?*
some: some people einige Leute [ine-ig-uh loy-tuh]
    may I have some? kann ich ein wenig bekommen? [kan ish ine vay-nish buh-kommen]
    may I have some grapes/some bread? kann ich ein paar Trauben/etwas Brot haben? [kan ish ine par trōw-ben/etvass broht hah-ben]
    may I have some more? darf ich noch ein wenig haben? [... nok ine vay-nish ...]
    that's some drink! das ist vielleicht ein Getränk! [dass ist fee-lysht ine gheh-trenk]
somebody jemand [yay-mannt]
something etwas [etvass]
sometime irgendwann [eer-ghent-van]
sometimes manchmal [manch-mal]
somewhere irgendwo [eer-ghent-voh]
son: my son mein Sohn [mine zohn]
song das Lied [leet]
soon bald [balt]
    as soon as possible so bald wie möglich [zoh balt vee murr-glish]
    sooner früher [frōō-er]
sore: it's sore es tut weh [ess toot vay]
sore throat das Halsweh [hallts-vay]
sorry: (I'm) sorry Entschuldigung! [ent-shool-digoong]
sort: this sort diese Art [dee-zuh art]
    what sort of ...? was für ein ...? [vass fōōr ine]
soup die Suppe [zoopp-uh]
sour sauer [zōw-er]
south der Süden [zōō-den]
souvenir ein Souvenir

104 SPACE HEATER

space heater ein Heizgerät
[... hites-gheh-rayt]
spade ein Spaten [shpaht-en]
Spain Spanien [shpahn-ee-en]
spare: spare part das Ersatzteil [air-zats-tile]
spare tire das Ersatzrad [−raht]
spark plug die Zündkerze [tsoont-kairtsuh]
speak: do you speak English? sprechen Sie
Englisch? [shpreshen zee eng-glish]
I don't speak ... ich kann kein ... [ish kan
kine]
special besonderer [buh-zon-der-rer]
special delivery (mail) per Expreß [pair
express]
specialist der Fachmann [fahk-man]
specially besonders [buh-zonders]
speed die Geschwindigkeit [gheh-shvin-dish-
kite]
he was speeding er ist zu schnell gefahren
[air ist tsoo shnell gheh-fahren]
speed limit die Geschwindigkeitsbegrenzung
[gheh-shvin-dik-kites-buh-grents-oong]
» *TRAVEL TIP: see* **drive**
speedometer der Tachometer [tak-o-may-ter]
Speisewagen dining car
spend (money) ausgeben [owss-gay-ben]
spice das Gewürz [gheh-voorts]
is it spicy? ist es stark gewürzt? [...
shtark ...]
spider die Spinne [shpin-uh]
spoon der Löffel [lurr-fel]
sprain: I've sprained it ich habe es mir
verstaucht [ish hah-buh ess meer fair-shtowkt]
Sprechstunden (of doctor) office hours
spring die Feder [fay-der]
(water) die Quelle [kvel-uh]
(season) der Frühling [froo-ling]
square (in town) der Platz
2 square meters 2 Quadratmeter [tsvy
kvad-raht-may-ter]
stairs die Treppe [trep-uh]
stale altbacken

STEP 105

stamp eine Briefmarke [breef-mark-uh]
 two stamps for America zwei Briefmarken nach Amerika [tsvy ... nahk am-ay-ree-kah]
stand stehen [shtay-en]
 (noun: at fair) der Stand [shtannt]
standard *(adjective)* normal [nor-mahl]
standby *(ticket)* Standby
star der Stern [shtairn]
starboard Steuerbord [shtoy-er-bort]
start der Anfang
 (of race) der Start [shtart]
 my car won't start mein Auto springt nicht an [mine ōwtoh shpringt nisht an]
 when does it start? wann fängt es an? [van fengt ess an]
starter *(car)* der Starter [shtarter]
starving: I'm starving ich habe einen Riesenhunger [ish hah-buh ine-en ree-zen-hoong-er]
state *(in country)* der Staat [shtaht]
 the States die Staaten
 in the States in den Staaten [... dayn ...]
station der Bahnhof [bahn-hohff]
statue die Statue [shtaht-oo-uh]
stay *(noun)* der Aufenthalt [ōwf-ent-hallt]
 we enjoyed our stay es hat uns hier gut gefallen [ess hat oons heer goot gheh-fal-en]
 I'm staying at ... ich wohne im ... [ish voh-nuh im]
 stay there bleiben Sie dort [bly-ben zee ...]
steak ein Steak [sht–]
 YOU MAY HEAR...
 wie möchten Sie Ihr Steak gebraten haben? – ganz durch, halb durch oder blutig? [... gants doorsh, halp doorsh oh-der blootish]
 how would you like your steak done? well done, medium or rare?
steep steil [shtile]
steering *(car)* die Lenkung [lenk-oong]
steering wheel das Steuerrad [shtoy-er-raht]
Stehplätze *standing room*
step *(noun)* die Stufe [shtoo-fuh]

stereo das Stereo
 (unit) die Stereoanlage [ster-ay-o-an-lah-guh]
stewardess die Stewardeß [–ess]
sticky klebrig [klay-brish]
stiff steif [shtife]
still: keep still bewegen Sie sich nicht
 [buh-vay-ghen zee zish nisht]
 I'm still here ich bin immer noch da
 [... nok ...]
stink (noun) der Gestank [gheh-shtank]
stolen: my wallet's been stolen man hat mir
 meine Brieftasche gestohlen
 [man hat meer mine-uh breef-tash-uh
 gheh-shtole-en]
stomach der Magen [mah-ghen]
 I have a stomach ache ich habe
 Magenschmerzen [ish hah-buh mah-ghen-
 shmairtsen]
 **have you got something for an upset
 stomach?** haben Sie etwas gegen
 Magenbeschwerden? [hah-ben zee etvass
 gay-ghen mah-ghen-buh-shvairden]
stone der Stein [shtine]
stop: stop! halt! [hallt]
 do you stop near...? halten Sie in der Nähe
 von...? [hal-ten zee in dair nay-uh fon]
stopover die Zwischenstation
 [tsvishen-shtats-ee-ohn]
store das Geschäft [gheh-shefft]
storm der Sturm [shtoorm]
strafbar: ... ist strafbar ... is an offence
stove der Herd [hairt]
straight gerade [gheh-rah-duh]
 go straight ahead gehen Sie geradeaus
 [gay-en zee gheh-rah-duh-ōwss]
 straight scotch Whisky pur [... poor]
straighten: will you straighten it out?
 können Sie das in Ordnung bringen? [kurrnen
 zee dass in ort-noong ...]
strange fremd [fremmt]
 (odd) seltsam [zelt-zahm]
stranger der Fremde [frem-duh]

I'm a stranger here ich bin fremd hier [ish bin fremmt heer]
strawberries Erdbeeren [airt-bair-en]
street die Straße [shtrahss-uh]
streetcar die Straßenbahn [shtrahssen-bahn]
string: do you have any string? haben Sie Schnur? [hah-ben zee shnoor]
stroke: he's had a stroke er hat einen Schlag(anfall) bekommen [air hat ine-en shlahg-an-fal buh-kommen]
stroller der Sportwagen [shport-vah-ghen]
strong stark [shtark]
student der Student [shtoo-dent]
(girl) die Studentin
stung: I've been stung ich bin gestochen worden [ish bin gheh-shtoken vorden]
stupid dumm [dœmm]
subway die Untergrundbahn, die U-Bahn [œnter-grœnt-bahn, oo-bahn]
suddenly plötzlich [plurrts-lish]
sugar der Zucker [tsœcker]
suit *(man's)* der Anzug [an-tsoog]
(woman's) das Kostüm [kostœm]
suitable passend [pas-ent]
suitcase der Koffer
summer der Sommer [zommer]
sun die Sonne [zonnuh]
  in the sun in der Sonne
  out of the sun im Schatten [shat-en]
sunbathe sonnenbaden [zonnen-bah-den]
sunburn der Sonnenbrand [zonnen-brannt]
Sunday Sonntag [zonn-tahg]
sunglasses die Sonnenbrille [zonnen-brill-uh]
suntan lotion das Sonnenöl [zonnen-urrl]
supermarket der Supermarkt [zooper--]
supper das Abendessen [ah-bent--]
sure: I'm not sure ich bin nicht sicher [ish bin nisht zisher]
  sure! sicher!
  are you sure? sind Sie sicher? [zinnt zee . . .]
surprise eine Überraschung [œber-rash-œng]

108 SWEARWORD

swearword der Fluch [flook]
sweat *(verb)* schwitzen [shvitsen]
sweater der Pullover
Sweden Schweden [shvay-den]
sweet süß [zōoss]
swerve: I had to swerve ich mußte ausschwenken [ish mooss-tuh ōwss-shvenken]
swim: I'm going for a swim ich gehe schwimmen [ish gay-uh shvimmen]
swimming pool das Schwimmbad [shvimm-baht]
swimsuit der Badeanzug [bah-duh-antsoog]
Swiss Schweizer [shvy-tser]
  (person) Schweizer
  (woman) Schweizerin
switch *(noun)* der Schalter [shall-ter]
  to switch on/off anschalten/abschalten [an-shall-ten /app–]
Switzerland die Schweiz [shvites]
  in Switzerland in der Schweiz
synagogue die Synagoge [zōo-na-go-guh]
table ein Tisch [tish]
  a table for 4 ein Tisch für vier [ine ... fōor feer]
table wine Tafelwein [tah-fel-vine]
take nehmen [nay-men]
  may I take this with me? kann ich das mitnehmen?
  will you take me to the airport? bringen Sie mich zum Flughafen? [... zee mish tsoom floog-hah-fen]
  how long will it take? wie lange dauert es? [vee lang-uh dōwert ess]
  somebody has taken my bags jemand hat mein Gepäck mitgenommen [yay-mannt hat mine gheh-peck mit-gheh-nommen]
  may I take you out tonight? kann ich Sie für heute abend einladen? [kan ish zee fōor hoy-tuh ah-bent ine-lah-den]
talcum powder der (Körper)puder [(kurr-per)pooder]

TELEPHONE 109

talk *(verb)* sprechen [shpreshen]
tall groß [grohss]
tampons die Tampons
tan die Bräune [broy-nuh]
tank *(of car)* der Tank
tap der Hahn
tape das Tonband [tohn-bannt]
tape recorder das Tonbandgerät [–gheh-rayt]
taste *(noun)* der Geschmack [geh-shm*a*ck]
  may I taste it? kann ich es versuchen? [kan ish ess fair-*zook*en]
  it tastes horrible/very good das schmeckt fürchterlich/sehr gut [dass shmeckt fōōrsh-terlish/zair goot]
taxi ein Taxi
  will you get me a taxi? rufen Sie mir, bitte, ein Taxi! [roofen zee meer bittuh . . .]
  where can I get a taxi? wo bekomme ich ein Taxi? [voh buh-k*o*mmuh ish . . .]
taxi driver der Taxifahrer
tea der Tee [tay]
  could I have a cup/pot of tea? könnte ich eine Tasse/ein Kännchen Tee haben? [kurrntuh ish ine-uh tass-uh/ine ken-shen tay hah-ben]
  YOU MAY THEN HEAR . . .
  mit Zitrone? *with lemon?*
  no, with milk, please nein, mit Milch, bitte [nine mit milsh bittuh]
teach: could you teach me? könnten Sie mir das beibringen? [kurrnten zee meer dass by-bringen]
  could you teach me German? könnten Sie mir Deutsch beibringen? [. . . doytsh . . .]
teacher der Lehrer [lair-ruh]
  (woman) die Lehrerin
telegram ein Telegramm
  I want to send a telegram ich möchte ein Telegramm schicken [ish murrshtuh . . .]
telephone *(noun)* das Telefon
  may I make a phone call? kann ich hier telefonieren? [. . . heer tele-fon*ee*r-en]

110 TELEVISION

may I speak to ...? kann ich ... sprechen? [... shpreshen]
could you get the number for me? könnten Sie die Nummer für mich wählen? [kurrnten zee dee noomer foor mish vay-len]
telephone directory das Telefonbuch [–book]
» *TRAVEL TIP: lift receiver, insert coin, dial; unused coins returned; for international calls look for boxes with green disk with 'Ausland' or 'International'; code for US and Canada is 001*

YOU MAY HEAR...
am Apparat *speaking*
Sie sind falsch verbunden *you've got the wrong number*
Augenblick bitte *one moment please*
kein Anschluß unter dieser Nummer *number no longer in use*
bitte warten *please wait*

television das Fernsehen [fairn-zay-en]
I'd like to watch television ich möchte gerne fernsehen [ish murrshtuh gairn-uh ...]
tell: could you tell me where ...? könnten Sie mir sagen, wo ...? [kurrnten zee meer zah-ghen voh]
temperature die Temperatur [–*toor*]
he has a temperature er hat Fieber [air hat feeber]
tennis Tennis
tennis ball der Tennisball [–bal]
tennis court der Tennisplatz
tennis racket der Tennisschläger [–shlay-gher]
tent das Zelt [tselt]
terminus die Endstation [ent-shtats-ee-ohn]
terrible schrecklich [shrecklish]
terrific sagenhaft [zah-ghen-haft]
than als [alts]
bigger/older than ... größer/älter als ... [grurrser/elter ...]
thanks, thank you danke(schön) [dank-uh(shurrn)]

THIN 111

no thank you nein danke [nine . . .]
thank you very much vielen Dank
[feelen . . .]
thank you for your help vielen Dank für Ihre
Hilfe [. . . foor eer-uh hilf-uh]
YOU MAY THEN HEAR . . .
bitteschön, bitte sehr *you're welcome*
that dieser, diese, dieses [deez-er, deez-uh, deez-es]
  that man/that table der Mann (dort)/der Tisch (dort)
  I'd like that one ich möchte das da [ish murrshtuh . . .]
  how do you say that? wie spricht man das aus? [vee shprisht man dass ōwss]
  I think that . . . ich glaube, daß . . . [ish glōw-buh dass]
the der, die, das
  (plural) die
theater das Theater [tay-*a*h-ter]
their ihr [eer]
  it's their bag/it's theirs das ist ihre Tasche/das ist ihre [. . . eer-uh . . .]
them sie [zee]
  with them mit ihnen [. . . een-en]
then dann
there dort
  how do I get there? wie komme ich dahin? [vee komm-uh ish dah-hin]
  is there/are there? gibt es? [gheept ess]
  there is/there are es gibt
  there you are *(giving something)* hier, bitte! [heer bittuh]
thermos die Thermosflasche [tairmos-flash-uh]
these diese [deez-uh]
they sie [zee]
  they are sie sind [zee zinnt]
thick dick
thief der Dieb [deep]
thigh der Schenkel [sh—]
thin dünn [dōōnn]

112 THING

thing das Ding
 I've lost all my things ich habe all meine Sachen verloren [ish hah-buh al mine-uh zah-ken fair-lor-ren]
think denken
 I'll think it over ich werde es mir überlegen [ish vair-duh ess meer ōober-lay-ghen]
 I think so/I don't think so ich denke schon/ich denke nicht [ish denk-uh shohn . . .]
third *(adjective)* dritte [drit-uh]
thirsty: I'm thirsty ich habe Durst [ish hah-buh dœrst]
this dieser, diese, dieses [deez-er, deez-uh, deez-es]
 may I have this one? kann ich das haben? [. . . dass hah-ben]
 this is my wife/this is Mr . . . (das ist) meine Frau/(das ist) Herr . . . [mine-uh frōw . . .]
 is this . . .? ist das . . .?
those diese (da) [deez-uh (dah)]
 those people diese Leute (da) [. . . loy-tuh . . .]
thread *(noun)* der Faden [fah-den]
throat der Hals [hallts]
throat lozenges Halspastillen [hallts–]
throttle der Gashebel [gahss-hay-bel]
through durch [dœrsh]
 Monday through Saturday von Montag bis Samstag [fon mohn-tahg biss zamz-tahg]
throw *(verb)* werfen [vair-fen]
thumb der Daumen [dōw-men]
thumbtack die Reißwecke [rice-tsveckuh]
thunder *(noun)* der Donner
thunderstorm ein Gewitter [gheh-vitter]
Thursday Donnerstag [donners-tahg]
ticket *(train)* die Fahrkarte [–kar-tuh]
 (bus) der Fahrschein [–shine]
 (plane) das Ticket
 (movie theater) die Eintrittskarte [ine-trits-kar-tuh]
 (checkroom) die Garderobenmarke [gar-duh-roh-ben-mark-uh]
» *TRAVEL TIP: see* **bus**

TIME 113

ticket office die Kasse [kass-uh]
tie *(necktie)* die Krawatte [krav-at-uh]
Tiefgarage underground parking
tight *(clothes)* eng
   they're too tight sie sind zu eng [zee zinnt tsoo ...]
time die Zeit [tsite]
   what time is it? wie spät ist es? [vee shpayt ist ess]
   I haven't got time ich habe keine Zeit [ish hah-buh kine-uh ...]
   for the time being vorläufig [for-loy-fish]
   this time/last time/next time dieses Mal/letztes Mal/nächstes Mal [deez-es mahl ...]
   3 times dreimal [dry-mahl]
   have a good time! viel Vergnügen! [feel fair-guh-no͞o-ghen]
» *TRAVEL TIP: how to tell the time*
   it's one o'clock es ist ein Uhr [... ine oor]
   it's 2/3/4/5/6 o'clock es ist zwei/drei/vier/fünf/sechs Uhr [tsvy/dry/feer/fo͞onf/zex oor]
   it's 5/10/20/25 after 7 es ist fünf/zehn/zwanzig/fünfundzwanzig (Minuten) nach sieben [fo͞onf/tsayn/ tsvan-tsish/fo͞onf-cont-tsvan-tsish nahk zeeben]
   it's quarter after 8/8:15 es ist Viertel nach acht/acht Uhr fünfzehn [feertel nahk ahkt/ahkt oor fo͞onf-tsayn]
   it's 9:30 es ist halb zehn/neun Uhr dreißig [halp tsayn/noyn oor dry-sish]
   it's 25/20 to ten es ist fünf/zehn nach halb zehn [fo͞onf/tsayn nahk halp tsayn]
   it's quarter to eleven es ist Viertel vor elf [feertel for elf]
   it's 10/5 to eleven es ist zehn/fünf (Minuten) vor elf [tsayn/fo͞onf for elf]
   it's twelve o'clock es ist zwölf (Uhr) [tsvurrlf]
   at ... um ... [oom]
» *TRAVEL TIP: notice that in German half past nine, etc. is said as 'half ten'!; in Germany the 24-hour clock system is used; 01:00 is one o'clock in the*

114 TIMETABLE

morning; 12:00 is noon; 16:00 is four o'clock in the afternoon; 24:00 is midnight
timetable *(travel)* der Fahrplan [–plahn]
tip *(gratuity)* das Trinkgeld [–gelt]
  is the tip included? ist das inklusive Bedienung? [ist dass in-kloo-zee-vuh buh-dee-noong]
» TRAVEL TIP: *tip same people as in US; also customary to tip in bars*
tire der Reifen [ry-fen]
  I need a new tire ich brauche einen neuen Reifen [ish brōwk-uh ine-en noy-en . . .]
» TRAVEL TIP: *tire pressures*
  lb/sq in. 18 20 22 24 26 28 30
  kg/sq cm 1.3 1.4 1.5 1.7 1.8 2 2.1
tired müde [mōō-duh]
  I'm tired ich bin müde [ish . . .]
tissues Papiertaschentücher [pa-peer-tashen-tōōk-er]
to: to America/Berlin nach Amerika/Berlin [nahk . . .]
toast der Toast
tobacco der Tabak
today heute [hoy-tuh]
toe die Zehe [tsay-he]
together zusammen [tsoo-zammen]
  we're together wir sind zusammen [veer zinnt . . .]
  can we pay all together? können wir alles zusammen bezahlen? [kurrnen veer al-ess . . . buh-tsah-len]
toilet die Toilette [twa-lettuh]
  there's no toilet paper es ist kein Toilettenpapier da [ess ist kine twa-letten-pa-peer dah]
» TRAVEL TIP: *see* **rest rooms**
tomato die Tomate [tomah-tuh]
  tomato juice der Tomatensaft [–zaft]
tomorrow morgen [mor-ghen]
  tomorrow morning/tomorrow afternoon/ tomorrow evening morgen früh/morgen nachmittag/morgen abend [. . . frōō]

TOURIST OFFICE 115

the day after tomorrow übermorgen [ōōber–]
see you tomorrow bis morgen
ton die Tonne [tonn-uh]
» *TRAVEL TIP: 1 ton = 907 kilos*
tongue die Zunge [tsoong-uh]
tonic water das Tonic (water)
tonight heute abend [hoy-tuh ah-bent]
tonsils die Mandeln
tonsillitis die Mandelentzündung
[–ent-tsōōn-dōōng]
too zu [tsoo]
(also) auch [ōwk]
that's too much das ist zuviel [dass ist tsoo-feel]
tool das Werkzeug [vairk-tsoyg]
tooth der Zahn [tsahn]
I have a toothache ich habe Zahnweh [ish hah-buh –vay]
toothbrush die Zahnbürste [tsahn-bōōrst-uh]
toothpaste die Zahnpasta [tsahn–]
top: on top of... auf [ōwf]
on the top floor im obersten Stock
at the top oben
topless oben ohne [oh-ben oh-nuh]
total *(noun)* die Endsumme [ent-zoom-uh]
tough *(meat)* zäh [tsay]
tour *(of area)* eine Rundreise [roont-ry-zuh]
(of town) ein Rundfahrt
(of castle) ein Rundgang
we'd like to go on a tour of... wir möchten gern eine Reise/eine Rundfahrt/einen Rundgang durch... machen [veer murrshten gairn...]
we're touring around wir reisen herum [veer ry-zen hair-oom]
tour guide der Reiseleiter [ry-zuh-ly-ter]
tourist der Tourist
I'm only a tourist ich bin fremd hier [ish bin fremmt heer]
tourist office das Fremdenverkehrsbüro
[frem-den-fair-kairs-bōō-roh]

116 TOW

tow *(verb)* abschleppen [app-shleppen]
 could you give me a tow? könnten Sie mich abschleppen? [kurrnten zee mish ...]
toward gegen [gay-ghen]
 he was coming straight toward me er kam geradewegs auf mich zu [air kahm gheh-rah-duh-veggs ōwf mish tsoo]
towel das Handtuch [hant-too*k*]
town die Stadt [shtat]
 in town in der Stadt
 would you take me into town? würden Sie mich in die Stadt bringen? [vōōrden zee ...]
towrope das Abschleppseil [app-shlep-zile]
track *(station):* **which track, please?** welches Gleis, bitte? [velshes glice bittuh]
traditional traditionell [tradi-tsee-oh-ne*l*]
 a traditional German meal ein echt deutsches Essen [ine esht doytshes ...]
traffic der Verkehr [fair-k*air*]
traffic circle der Kreisverkehr [krice-fair-kair]
traffic light die Ampel
trailer der Wohnwagen [vohn-vah-ghen]
train der Zug [tsoog]
» *TRAVEL TIP: efficient and punctual; if you travel between cities by express (Intercity) you'll have to buy a surcharge ticket (Zuschlag* [tsoo-shlahg]*); it's cheaper to buy this before you get on the train*
 YOU MAY HEAR ...
 noch jemand zugestiegen? *any more tickets, please?*
tranquillizers Beruhigungsmittel [buh-roo-ig∞ngs-]
transformer ein Trafo [trah-foh]
translate übersetzen [ōōber-zet-sen]
 would you translate that for me? würden Sie das für mich übersetzen? [vōōrden zee dass fōōr mish ...]
transmission *(of car)* das Getriebe [gheh-tr*ee*-buh]
travel agency das Reisebüro [ry-zuh-bōō-roh]
traveler's check der Travellerscheck
tree der Baum [bōwm]

trip *(noun)* die Reise [ry-zuh]
(outing) der Ausflug [ōwss-floog]
  we want to go on a trip to ... wir möchten nach ... fahren [veer murrsh-ten nahk ...]
  have a good trip gute Reise! [goo-tuh ...]
trouble die Schwierigkeiten [shvee-rish-kite-en]
  I'm having trouble with ... ich habe Schwierigkeiten mit ... [ish hah-buh ...]
trousers die Hose [hoh-zuh]
truck der Last(kraft)wagen, der Lkw [lasst(krafft)vah-ghen, el-kah-vay]
truck driver der Lkw-Fahrer
true wahr [vahr]
  it's not true das ist nicht wahr [dass ist nisht ...]
trunk *(of car)* der Kofferraum [–rōwm]
trunks *(swimming)* die Badehose [bah-duh-hoh-zuh]
trust: I trust you ich vertraue Ihnen [ish fair-trōw-uh een-en]
try *(verb)* versuchen [fair-zook-en]
  may I try it on? kann ich es anprobieren? [kan ish ess an-proh-bee-ren]
T-shirt das T-shirt
Tuesday Dienstag [deenz-tahg]
tunnel der Tunnel
turn: where do we turn off? wo biegen wir ab? [voh bee-ghen veer app]
  he turned without signaling er bog ab, ohne Zeichen zu geben [air bohg app oh-nuh tsy-shen tsoo gay-ben]
  may I have a turn? kann ich es versuchen? [kan ish ess fair-zoo-ken]
twice zweimal [tsvy-mal]
  twice as much doppelt soviel [... zoh-feel]
twin beds zwei (Einzel)betten [tsvy (ine-tsel)–]
typewriter die Schreibmaschine [shripe-mash-ee-nuh]
typical typisch [tōō-pish]
U-Bahn subway
ugly häßlich [hess-lish]

118 ULCER

ulcer das Geschwür [geh-shv $\overline{oo}$ r]
umbrella der Schirm [sheerm]
Umleitung detour
uncle: my uncle mein Onkel
uncomfortable unbequem [oon-buh-kvaym]
unconscious bewußtlos [buh-v ∞ st-lohss]
under unter [oonter]
underage minderjährig [minnder-yair-rik]
underdone *(not cooked)* nicht gar [nisht . . .]
understand: I understand ich verstehe [ish fair-sht*a*y-uh]
  I don't understand das verstehe ich nicht
  do you understand? verstehen Sie? [fair-sht*a*y-en zee]
undo aufmachen [ōwf-mah-*k*en]
unfriendly unfreundlich [oon-froynt-lish]
unhappy unglücklich [oon-gl $\overline{oo}$ ck-lish]
United States die Vereinigten Staaten [dee fair-*i*ne-ish-ten shtah-ten]
unlock aufschließen [ōwf-shlee-sen]
until bis
  not until Tuesday nicht vor Dienstag [nisht for . . .]
unusual ungewöhnlich [oon-gheh-vurrn-lish]
up: up in the mountains oben in den Bergen
  he's not up yet er ist noch nicht auf [air ist no*k* nisht ōwf]
upside-down verkehrt herum [fair-k*ai*rt hair-oom]
upstairs oben
urgent dringend [dring-ent]
us uns [oonts]
  it's us wir sind's [veer zinnts]
use: may I use . . . ? kann ich . . . benutzen? [kan ish buh-n*oo*t-sen]
useful nützlich [n $\overline{oo}$ ts-lish]
usual(ly) gewöhnlich [gheh-v*u*rrn-lish]
  as usual wie gewöhnlich [vee . . .]
U-turn die Wende [ven-duh]
vacancy ein (freies) Zimmer
  do you have any vacancies? haben Sie noch Zimmer frei? [hah-ben zee no*k* tsimmer fry]

WAIST 119

vacate *(room)* räumen [roy-men]
vacation der Urlaub [oor-lōwp]
  (student's) die Ferien [fay-ree-en]
  I'm on vacation ich bin im Urlaub/in Ferien
vaccination die Impfung [imp-foong]
valid gültig [gōōlti*k*]
  how long is it valid for? wie lange gilt es?
  [vee lang-uh ghilt ess]
valley das Tal [tahl]
valuable wertvoll [vairt-fol]
value *(noun)* der Wert [vairt]
valve das Ventil [ven-*tee*l]
vanilla Vanille [van-*ee*-luh]
varicose veins die Krampfadern [–ah-dern]
veal das Kalbfleisch [kalp-flysh]
vegetables Gemüse [gheh-m*ōō*-zuh]
vegetarian *(noun)* ein Vegetarier [vay-gheh-t*a*r-ee-er]
ventilator der Ventilator [–l*a*h-tor]
verboten *forbidden*
very sehr [zair]
via über [*ōō*ber]
village das Dorf
vine die Rebe [ray-buh]
vinegar der Essig [–ish]
vineyard der Weinberg [vine-bairk]
vintage der Jahrgang [yahr–]
violent heftig [–ish]
visa ein Visum [vee-zoom]
visibility die Sicht [zisht]
visit *(verb)* besuchen [buh-*zook*-en]
vodka der Wodka [v–]
voice die Stimme [shtim-uh]
voltage die Spannung [shpan-oong]
» *TRAVEL TIP: voltage is 220 AC*
Vorsicht! *caution*
Vorsicht, bissiger Hund *beware of the dog*
Vorsicht Stufe *mind the step*
waist die Taille [ty-uh]
» *TRAVEL TIP: waist measurements*

US	24	26	28	30	32	34	36	38
Germany	61	66	71	76	80	87	91	97

120 WAIT

wait: will we have to wait long? müssen wir lange warten? [mōossen veer lang-uh varten]
  wait for me warten Sie auf mich [... zee ōwf mish]
  I'm waiting for a friend ich warte auf einen Freund [ish var-tuh ōwf ine-en froynt]
waiter der Kellner
  waiter! (Herr) Ober!
waitress die Kellnerin
  waitress! Fräulein! [froy-line]
wake: will you wake me up at 7:30? wecken Sie mich, bitte, um 7.30 [vecken zee mish bittuh oom halp ah*k*t]
walk: can we walk there? können wir zu Fuß hingehen? [kurrnen veer tsoo fooss hin-gay-en]
walking shoes die Wanderschuhe [vander-shoo-uh]
wall die Mauer [mōwer]
  (inside) die Wand [vannt]
wallet die Brieftasche [breef-tash-uh]
want: I want a ... ich möchte ein ... [ish murrshtuh]
  I want to talk to ... ich möchte mit ... sprechen
  what do you want? was möchten Sie? [vass murrshten zee]
  I don't want to ich will nicht [ish vill nisht]
  he wants to ... er will ... [air vill]
  they don't want to sie wollen nicht
warm warm [varm]
warning die Warnung [varn-oong]
was: I was/he was/it was ich war/er war/es war [... var]
Wartesaal *waiting room*
wash: can you wash these for me? könnten Sie diese für mich waschen? [kurrnten zee dee-zuh fōor mish vashen]
  where can I wash ...? wo kann ich ... waschen? [voh ...]
washer *(for bolt, etc.)* die Dichtung [dish-toong]
washing machine die Waschmaschine [vash-mash-een-uh]

WEEK 121

wasp die Wespe [vesp-uh]
watch *(wrist-)* die (Armband)uhr
 [(armbannt)oor]
  will you watch ... for me? würden Sie für
  mich auf ... aufpassen? [vōorden zee fōor mish
  ōwf ... ōwf-pas-en]
  watch out! Achtung! [ah*k*-tōong]
water das Wasser [vasser]
  may I have some water? darf ich Wasser
  haben? [... ish hah-ben]
waterfall der Wasserfall [vasser-fal]
waterproof wasserdicht [vasser-disht]
waterskiing Wasserskilaufen
 [vasser-shee-lōwfen]
way: we'd like to eat the German way wir
 möchten gerne typisch deutsch essen [veer
 murrsh-ten gairn-uh tōopish doytsh essen]
  could you tell me the way to ...?
  könnten Sie mir den Weg nach ... sagen?
  [kurrnten zee meer dayn vayg
  nah*k* ... zah-ghen]
  see **where** *for answers*
we wir [veer]
  we are wir sind [veer zinnt]
weak schwach [shvah*k*]
weather das Wetter [v–]
  what terrible weather! so ein Sauwetter!
  [zoh ine zōw–]
  what's the weather forecast? was sagt der
  Wetterbericht? [vass zahgt dair –buh-risht]
  YOU MAY THEN HEAR...
  überwiegend heiter *generally fine*
  leichte/schwere Schauer *light/heavy showers*
  Gewitter *thundery*
  sonnig, warm, kalt *sunny, warm, cold*
Wednesday Mittwoch [mit-vo*k*]
week die Woche [vock-uh]
  a week from today/tomorrow heute/morgen
  in einer Woche [hoy-tuh/mor-ghen in
  ine-er ...]
  on the weekend am Wochenende [am
  vocken-end-uh]

122 WEIGHT

weight das Gewicht [geh-visht]
welcome: you're welcome bitte sehr [bittuh zair]
well: I'm not feeling well ich fühle mich nicht wohl [ish fool-uh mish nisht vole]
   he's not well es geht ihm nicht gut [ess gayt eem nisht goot]
   how are you? – very well, thanks wie geht's? – danke, gut! [vee gayts dankuh goot]
   you speak English very well Sie sprechen sehr gut Englisch [zee spreshen zair goot eng-glish]
were: you were Sie waren [zee varen] *(familiar)* du warst [doo varst]
   you were *(plural)* Sie waren; *(familiar)* ihr wart [eer vart] *see* **you**
   we were wir waren [veer ...]
   they were sie waren
west der Westen [v–]
wet naß [nass]
what was [vass]
   what is that? was ist das?
   what for? wozu? [voh-tsoo]
   what room? welches Zimmer? [velshes tsimmer]
wheel das Rad [raht]
wheelchair der Rollstuhl [rol-shtool]
when wann [van]
   when I arrived als ich ankam [alts ish an-kahm]
where wo [voh]
   where is the post office? wo ist das Postamt?
   YOU MAY THEN HEAR...
   geradeaus *straight ahead*
   erste Querstraße links/rechts *first left/right*
   an der Ampel vorbei *past the traffic light*
which welcher, welche, welches? [velsher ...]
   which one? welcher?
   YOU MAY THEN HEAR...
   dieser, diese, dieses [deezer ...] *this one*
   der da, die da, das da *that one*
   der, die, das linke/rechte *the one on the left/right*

WINE 123

white weiß [vice]
who wer [vair]
whose wessen [vessen]
  whose is this? wem gehört das? [vaym geh-hurrt dass]
  YOU MAY THEN HEAR...
  (das gehört) ihm/ihr/mir *(it belongs)* to *him/her/me*
why warum [varoom]
  why not? warum nicht? [...nisht]
wide weit [vite]
wife: my wife meine Frau [mine-uh frōw]
will: when will it be finished? wann ist es fertig? [van ist ess fairtish]
  will you do it? tun Sie es? [toon zee ess]
  I will come back ich komme wieder [ish komm-uh veeder]
win *(verb)* gewinnen [geh-vinnen]
  who won? wer hat gewonnen? [vair...]
wind *(noun)* der Wind [vinnt]
window das Fenster
  near the window am Fenster
windshield die Windschutzscheibe [vinnt-shoots-shy-buh]
windshield wipers die Scheibenwischer [shy-ben-visher]
windsurfing das Windsurfen [vinnt-zurrfen]
windy windig [vindish]
wine der Wein [vine]
  may I see the wine list? kann ich die Getränkekarte haben? [kan ish dee geh-trenkuh-kartuh hah-ben]
» *TRAVEL TIP: mainly white wines (Weißwein [vice-vine]); fewer reds (Rotwein [roht-vine]); three quality grades –* **Tafelwein** *is a table wine without a named vineyard;* **Qualitätswein** *is quality wine from a designated region;* **Qualitätswein mit Prädikat** *is special quality wine; there are countless varieties; some of the main grapes are:* **Riesling** *medium dry;*

124 WINTER

Sylvaner *dry;* **Gutedel** *very dry;* **Müller-Thurgau**
light, fruity; **Ruländer** *full-bodied, sweetish;*
Traminer *full-bodied, strong;* **Weißherbst,**
Schiller *fruity rosés (Rosé)*

winter der Winter [v–]
wire der Draht
   (elec.) die Leitung [ly-toong]
wish: best wishes alles Gute
with mit
without ohne [oh-nuh]
witness ein Zeuge [tsoy-guh]
   will you act as a witness for me? würden Sie
   mein Zeuge sein? [vōorden zee mine . . . zine]
woman die Frau [frōw]
   women die Frauen [frōwen]
wonderful herrlich [hair-lish]
won't: it won't start es springt nicht an [ess
shpringt nisht an]
wood das Holz
woods der Wald [valt]
wool die Wolle [vol-uh]
word das Wort [vort]
   I don't know that word ich kenne das Wort
nicht [ish kenn-uh dass . . . nisht]
work *(verb)* arbeiten [ar-by-ten]
   it's not working es funktioniert nicht [ess
foonk-tsee-oh-neert nisht]
   I work in New York ich arbeite in New York
[ish ar-by-tuh . . .]
worry die Sorge [zor-guh]
   I'm worried about him ich mache mir Sorgen
um ihn [ish mah-*k*uh meer zor-ghen oom een]
   don't worry keine Sorge [kine-uh . . .]
worse: it's worse es ist schlimmer [. . . shl–]
   he's getting worse es geht ihm schlechter [ess
gayt eem shleshter]
worst schlechteste [shlesht-est-uh]
worth: it's not worth that much so viel ist es
nicht wert [zoh feel ist ess nisht vairt]
   is it worthwhile going to . . .? lohnt es sich,
nach . . . zu gehen? [. . . zish nah*k* . . . tsoo
gay-en]

wrap: could you wrap it up? könnten Sie es einpacken? [kurrnten zee ess ine–]
wrapping paper das Packpapier [pack-pap*ee*r]
wrench *(noun: tool)* der Schraubenschlüssel [shrōwben-shlōōsel]
wrist das Handgelenk [hannt-geh–]
write schreiben [shryben]
  could you write it down? könnten Sie das aufschreiben? [kurrnten zee dass ōwf-shryben]
  I'll write to you ich schreibe Ihnen [ish shry-buh een-en]
writing paper das Schreibpapier [shryp-pap*ee*r]
wrong falsch [falsh]
  I think the check's wrong ich glaube, die Rechnung stimmt nicht [ish glōw-buh dee resh-n*oo*ng shtimmt nisht]
  there's something wrong with ... da stimmt etwas nicht mit ... [... etvass ...]
  what's wrong? was ist los? [vass ist lohss]
  you're wrong Sie irren sich [zee irren zish]
  sorry, wrong number tut mir leid, falsch verbunden [toot meer lite falsh fair-b*oo*nden]
X-ray die Röntgenaufnahme [rurrnt-ghen-ōwf-nah-muh]
yacht die Jacht [yah*k*t]
yard *(garden)* der Garten
  » *TRAVEL TIP: 1 yard = 91.44 cm = 0.91 m*
year das Jahr [y–]
yellow gelb [ghelp]
yes ja [yah]
  you can't – yes, I can Sie können das nicht – doch! [zee kurrnen dass nisht – do*k*]
yesterday gestern [ghestern]
  the day before yesterday vorgestern [for–]
  yesterday morning/afternoon/evening gestern morgen/nachmittag/abend
yet: is it ready yet? ist es fertig? [ist ess *fairtik*]
  not yet noch nicht [no*k* nisht]
yogurt ein Joghurt

126 YOU

you Sie [zee]; *(familiar)* du [doo]
(plural) Sie [zee]; *(familiar)* ihr [eer]
   are you...? sind Sie.../bist du...? [zinnt zee...]
   I like you ich mag Sie/dich/euch [ish mahg zee/dish/oysh]
   with you mit Ihnen/dir/euch [mit eenen/dir/oysh]
» *TRAVEL TIP: use the 'Sie' forms in most situations; the 'du' forms are only for people you know well*
young jung [yœng]
your Ihr [eer]; *(familiar)* dein [dine]
(familiar plural) euer [oy-er]
   is this yours? ist es Ihrer/deiner?
youth hostel die Jugendherberge [yoo-ghent-hair-bair-guh]
» *TRAVEL TIP: only Bavaria has an age limit of 27*
Yugoslavia Jugoslawien [yoogo-slahv-ee-en]
Zentrum center
zero Null [nœl]
   below zero unter Null [œnter...]
ziehen pull
Zimmer frei vacancy, rooms
zipper der Reißverschluß [rice-fair-shlœoss]
Zoll Customs
Zutritt verboten no admission
zu verkaufen for sale
zu vermieten for rent

ALPHABET 127

The German alphabet

a [ah]
b [bay]
c [tsay]
d [day]
e [ay]
f [eff]
g [gay]
h [hah]
i [ee]
j [yot]
k [kah]
l [el]
m [em]
n [en]
o [oh]
p [pay]
q [koo]
r [air]
s [ess]
t [tay]
u [oo]
v [fōw]
w [vay]
x [eeks]
y [ōop-zee-lon]
z [tset]
ß = ss

NUMBERS

- 0 null [nool]
- 1 eins [ine-ts]
- 2 zwei [tsvy]
- 3 drei [dry]
- 4 vier [feer]
- 5 fünf [foonf]
- 6 sechs [zex]
- 7 sieben [zeeben]
- 8 acht [ah*k*t]
- 9 neun [noyn]
- 10 zehn [tsayn]
- 11 elf
- 12 zwölf [tsvurrlf]
- 13 dreizehn [dry-tsayn]
- 14 vierzehn
- 15 fünfzehn
- 16 sechzehn
- 17 siebzehn [zeep–]
- 18 achtzehn
- 19 neunzehn
- 20 zwanzig [tsvan-tsish]
- 21 einundzwanzig [ine-oont–]
- 22 zweiundzwanzig
- 23 dreiundzwanzig
- 24 vierundzwanzig
- 25 fünfundzwanzig
- 26 sechsundzwanzig
- 27 siebenundzwanzig
- 28 achtundzwanzig
- 29 neunundzwanzig
- 30 dreißig [dry-sish]
- 31 einunddreißig

- 40 vierzig
- 50 fünfzig
- 60 sechzig
- 70 siebzig [zeep–]
- 80 achtzig
- 90 neunzig

- 100 hundert [hoondert]
- 101 hunderteins
- 175 hundertfünfundsiebzig [hoondert-foonf-oont-zeep-tsish]
- 200 zweihundert
- 1,000 tausend [tow-zent]
- 2,000 zweitausend
- 1,000,000 eine Million [ine-uh mil-ee-yone]

The Germans use a comma as a decimal point; for thousands use a period, as in 2.000.

ABCDEF